HONORARY CONSUL PATTAYA

HONORARY CONSUL PATTAYA

Barry Kenyon
January 2014

An exploration of the British honorary consul's activities in Pattaya, Thailand, dealing with troubled Brits during fourteen action-packed years working for the British embassy in Bangkok.

HONORARY CONSUL PATTAYA
By Barry Kenyon
Copyright 2014 Barry Kenyon
Front cover by Richard C. Plaza
Layout by Siamese Vision Media Co., Ltd.
This edition is printed by Prechathon Interprint Co., Ltd.
4/5 Soi Ramintra 42 Yak 8, Ramintra Rd., Kwaeng Ramintra, Kannayaw, Bangkok 10230

ISBN: 978-616-348-995-1

"Nobody visits Pattaya to enjoy the waterfalls" (Pattaya police chief)

Prologue

I decided to write this book whilst I was banged up in the Pattaya police station holding cells. I should explain my sojourn there lasted one night and was purely voluntary. It was part of the self-chosen training I gave myself as the British embassy's consular representative in this neck of the woods. The cells were overcrowded and I spent most of the night crushing ants and watching a Thai ladyboy calmly painting her nails and pinching her facial pimples with the help of a small mirror and a pair of pincers.

I have always believed that you fulfil a role best if you have some experience, however limited, of what other people are going through. By the morning I was stiff in every joint, badly in need of a shower and felt as if I had been eaten alive by a miscellany of tiny, winged creatures. The police officer on duty who let me out said I must be completely mad as he offered me the remains of his cheese sandwich which I noticed was laced with sickly-sweet Carnation milk, Thai style. I have never understood why Thais mostly avoid becoming fat in view of their addiction to sugar.

It is generously added to most rice and noodle dishes and carbonated drinks in Thailand always seem to taste much sweeter than in England.

I was the British embassy's Pattaya representative for 13 years from 1997 with a variety of titles, but latterly acting as honorary consul which, contrary to common belief, does carry a modest annual stipend (about two thousand pounds) and travel expenses. For the most part, the experience was an enjoyable one which is why there is an element of humour, even idiosyncrasy, in the chapters which follow. But there were times of disappointment and stress which I have not sought to avoid whenever relevant.

Although personal details crop up here and there, this book is not an autobiography. If it was, the list of characters would be vastly different. I should also say that the Thai libel laws, criminal as well as civil in this country, are very easy to invoke. It is true that I have omitted a few controversial matters and individuals if only because I am not an unduly rich man and don't feel like fighting tedious court battles for the rest of this decade by which time I shall have reached my eighties. The slowness of the Thai judicial system means that legal battles can last more than 10 years.

The famous journalist and blogger Andrew Drummond figures here and there in the chapters which follow. Andrew, whom I have met only a handful of times over the years, is a Scots-born investigative journalist based in Bangkok to whom many expats in Thailand owe a great deal whether they know it or not. He has specialized in exposing some of the scams and crimes which foreigners allegedly have perpetrated on other foreigners in the Land of Smiles. Admittedly controversial in his internet blog, he has never (at the time of writing) lost a legal battle in which he was the defendant in a civil or criminal action. He has a lot to say about Pattaya and is not the sort of guy to decline to call a spade a spade. It is very easy to find his website and those of his vociferous opponents on Google. By all means read both sides and make up your own mind. No wonder Andrew's score produces well over 600,000 monthly internet hits.

Although I retired from British embassy responsibilities in 2010, my role directly and indirectly dragged on until 2013 as you can read in one of the later chapters. This largely explains why it has taken until 2014 to publish this account. I still receive regular phone calls asking for consular assistance of one sort and another, probably because I never bothered to change my private phone number. But I don't get involved in other people's problems these days. In any case, the British embassy's role is continually changing owing to financial cuts imposed in London and front-line services for troubled Brits are decidedly on the wane.

A number of people have kindly read through parts of the manuscript, but my biggest debt of gratitude is to two Manchester guys, Colin Thomas and Bob Splaine, who provided me with firm friendship and solid support during the years when I was in office.

Both were regular visitors to Thailand – Bob was married to a Thai – and they were invariably pillars of strength when I ran into personal problems arising from my public role which I did from time to time. Sadly, both died of heart trouble far too early in their mid-50s. However, I dedicate Honorary Consul Pattaya for their memory. Requiescant in Pace.

Barry Kenyon

Pattaya, January 2014

Contents

PROLOGUE	7
ONE: PATTAYA'S POTTED PAST	13
TWO: BOOMS AND SLUMPS	20
THREE: QUEEN VICTORIA'S STATUE	29
FOUR: BRITS IN THE SHITS	36
FIVE: THE GRIM REAPER	45
SIX: THAT'S YOUR FUNERAL	54
SEVEN: PLAYING DOCTORS AND NURSES	61
EIGHT: THE TRAGIC AND THE BIZARRE	69
NINE: THE RED LIGHT DISTRICT	78
TEN: SPRINGTIME FOR HITLER	88
ELEVEN: BE UPSTANDING IN COURT	96
TWELVE: HELL WITH COLIN MARTIN	105
THIRTEEN: THE POLITICIAN'S BAGMAN	113
FOURTEEN: THE CONTRACT KILLER	121
FIFTEEN: MBE AND PEDOPHILIA	129
SIXTEEN: READ ALL ABOUT IT	138
SEVENTEEN: BODY SNATCHERS AND THE COUP	147
EIGHTEEN: HAVE YOUR PASSPORT READY	155
NINETEEN: DECLINE AND FALL	163
TWENTY: PREMATURE BURIAL	171
TWENTY ONE: ROUND THE WORLD WITH PAPA DOC	183
AFTERWORD	191

ONE: PATTAYA'S POTTED PAST

Pattaya today is a concrete jungle but still a fascinating one. Although the Thais are certainly in charge, the city manages to maintain the illusion that it's run by foreigners. You hear British newsreaders on the local cable TV and on the radio. There are Russian business signs in every street and Russian restaurant menus wherever you go. The better-class hospitals have foreign interpreters to reassure you or even tell you what's wrong with you medically. The different sections of the police have foreign volunteers in various roles. If you fancy a drag show in a club, you will almost certainly find British men in frocks singing rude shanties. There are foreigners running, or seeming to run, go-go bars, car hire firms, estate agencies, visa and bucket shops and even law firms. And, of course, the city boasts a goodly number of foreign conmen and criminals who know how to play the Thai system of rules and regulations.

It wasn't always like this. Given Pattaya's international fame, it's perhaps surprising that the resort's local history is a more or less total blank. Pattaya may be the biggest urban sprawl in the world without a recorded or written-up past.

Very few archaeologists have bothered to dig here and all have given up in despair on finding nothing but sand and rock. As regards who was living here for all of ancient and medieval history, and most of modern times, we haven't the slightest idea.

An American anthropologist explained to me recently that he had written four volumes on the ancient tribes of Papua Guinea but could only provide a blank piece of paper when considering Pattaya's past.

However, it is clear that Pattaya began life as a fishing village centuries ago. That fact is still obvious today if you look across the local bay after the sun goes down and watch the trawlers setting out to deeper waters to bring ashore a marine catch. Next door is the non-touristy town of Naklua where the stretched-out fishing nets and allied paraphernalia are still the main attractions for the sauntering visitor. Luckily, in recent years, the Pattaya local authority has spent a small fortune cleaning up the polluted beaches in Naklua. Now you can actually see fish swimming in the bay rather than lying dead on the surface. That's progress, of course, as well as being one of the district's few environmental triumphs.

History becomes a little clearer in the eighteenth century. The Thai king Taksin the Great (1734-1782) of Chinese heritage, not to be confused with a later and controversial prime minister of our own times, succeeded much to his own surprise at turning back, at a place called Pad Tai Ya, the hostile invading Burmese army which had just sacked the city of Ayudthaya upcountry and were trying to carry away any new booty they could lay their hands on.

It is not altogether clear whether there was a pitched battle or whether the Burmese decided to throw in the towel because their leaders were in a drunken stupor. But legend insists that some kind of hostility occurred at what is now Thepprasit Road, a major thoroughfare dividing Pattaya from the nearby resort of

Jomtien. Anyway, the Burmese retreated and the hero Taksin the Great is still commemorated by an impressive statue at the gates of Pattaya's City Hall.

Taksin, who incidentally was the first Thai ruler to suffer a military coup in his comparative old age, was also the royal initiator of trading with the British who were based in imperial India at the time. In 1776 George Stratton, the viceroy of Madras, sent Taksin a group of military trainers and 1,400 flintlock guns which in due course led to a booming business for British arms manufacturers throughout the entire region. No wonder a grateful British government then sent Taksin the gift of a gold scabbard decorated with precious gems.

Let's move forward. In 2005 a European guy was preparing to install a grandiose swimming pool in his rented villa near Thepprasit Road. Knowing something about the Burmese debacle, he decided to excavate the ground or, to be absolutely truthful, to watch the workmen turning over the sod as foreigners are not allowed to work in the fields with or without a work permit. Initially it did appear that history was in the making as two rusty relics were unearthed which were thought to belong to pre-history. Disappointingly, one turned out to be an obsolete tin hat and the other part of a bazooka belonging to the Second World War era. They were probably Japanese.

If you want a glimpse today of the eastern seaboard, of which Pattaya is a part, then take a 50 minutes' drive to Plutaluang golf course located near the provincial airport of U-tapao. The airport itself became famous in late 2008 for the emergency airlifts of stranded passengers after Bangkok's Suvarnabhumi airport was closed by the yellow shirts who were trying to bring down the government of the day. These days, U-tapao's main commercial role is to play host to tourist charter flights, principally from the former Soviet Union, as well as to some scheduled flights.

However, there are government plans to make U-tapao into a major aviation hub on top of its subsidiary role of acting as a repair and servicing facility for the Thai Airways fleet. These plans are currently being resisted by the airport owners, The Royal Thai Navy, on the grounds that they need the bulk of the airport's available land for training military personnel.

Near the Plutaluang golf course you can still see several villas, some crumbling and some restored, where American pilots were based for their bombing runs to Vietnam and Cambodia in the early 1970s whilst president Nixon struggled to save his reputation in an unwinnable war. U-tapao still has one of the longest runways in Asia, built specifically half a century ago to facilitate the heavy bombers taking off with their deadly explosives and napalm. U-tapao has now largely forgotten its wartime history which is just as well.

In one of those villas today lives Ray, an American ex-serviceman, who lives with his Thai wife Noi and several of the extended kin as is common in traditional Thai families. Now in his 70s, Ray is one of those stalwart émigrés who decided not to return to the United States once Saigon and Phnom Penh fell to the communist insurgents in 1975. He says he does not wish to be properly identified as he has not filled in a tax form for years and still fears the American internal revenue service. He also has an overstay visa for Thailand in his passport which does not remotely worry him. He says if he ever leaves the Land of Smiles it will be in a pine box. Every few months he drops off a bottle of Black Label at the local police station. That's OK he says.

There are a few other old timers from the 1970s still alive and kicking in the Pattaya area. One Brit we'll call Andy still runs a bar in the resort although he says business is bad since the British pound sank in 2013 after a long and painful decline. By early 2014 it had recovered a bit thanks to a violent political crisis facing the government in Bangkok, but tourists were thin on the ground. Andy is trying to sell the bar and return to Salford. "Bombs, demos and talk of military coups are killers of the tourist industry," he laments.

For years Andy was obsessed with keeping his surname a secret, even from his Thai wife. This strategy is well known amongst Brits who either think, or are indeed positive, they are being sought by the British police for some historical misdemeanor and believe that Pattaya is a safe bolt-hole. The farce about his identity continued for some years until a customer showed him a recent copy of a local newspaper with his full name and photo prominently displayed on the sports pages. Unfortunately, Andy was a very good golfer and the local press traditionally reports local matches on a week-by-week basis. His real name was known because he had had to show his passport to the golf club authorities when he originally took out membership. The lesson of this seems to be that you must avoid holes-in-one and birdies if you wish to avoid being exposed by a watchful media. Andy still runs the bar and Interpol never did show up. But golf is a banned subject on the high stools near to where he still sits sipping imported whisky on the rocks.

As a seaside resort, Pattaya began to take off in the 1960s. The first holidaymakers were mainly Thais from Bangkok, with their own transport, who started the tradition of weekend picnics in the still rural Pattaya to enjoy the freshness of the sea and a dose of tranquility. Even today you can still see grandma and the kids piling into the back of a pickup late on Sunday afternoon as they head back to the metropolis, a mere two hours away by the newly constructed motorway. It's not unknown for elderly Thais from the northern provinces to visit Pattaya for the first time in their lives and just stare at the ocean which they have never seen before. Part of the magic of Thailand is that it is truly a mixture: traditional and naïve in some ways whilst being increasingly cosmopolitan and greedy in others.

As the number of foreign visitors grew, the opportunities to make money jumped by leaps and bounds. Young Thai ladies, mostly from the impoverished Isaan region of northern Thailand, flocked to Pattaya to befriend the American military personnel who were hungry for a good time whilst on leave. This particular tradition has survived until today and the annual Cobra Gold military exercises in Thailand, coupled with periodic visits by American aircraft carriers and destroyers, are eagerly anticipated by the resort's business owners and their employees with cash tills at the ready. However, these days the American sailors must do a spot of social work during their long weekend break and are seen in large numbers, paintbrushes in hand, refurbishing a classroom or repainting a monastery toilet in the cause of international public relations. Such is the role that the flag-bearers of western democracy must bear in the 21st century. It is also their lot to contribute to saving the environment by cleaning up in increasingly polluted Asia.

Hotels by the night or by the hour began to spring up to cater for the madding crowd and, by the 1970s, Walking Street was beginning to take shape with its tailor shops, burger joints, open bars and nightclubs galore. Pattaya was gearing up to become one of the world's international hot spots for sea, sand and sex. A Thai saying of the time quipped, "If you want to see a naked foreigner, then go to Pattaya." In other words it's full of farang trash! Farang is an anglicized Thai word for foreigner, although it is not always meant in a disparaging way. You'll meet the expression often in this book.

From the beginning a determined attempt was made to cater for all tastes. Some of the good-time girls even sported tattoos on their more intimate parts proclaiming "Welcome US Marines" or "I'm More Comfortable Lying Down". The bars and nightclubs began to grace themselves with suggestive names in gaudy neon, a tradition which has survived to this day. There was Bar 69, Purring Pussy, Titty Palace, Cockatoo, Shagaroo and so on. There was even one brave soul who renamed his bar Fuck Off Two, a rebranding deemed necessary because he was doing poor business with Fuck Off One. That was a step too far even for Pattaya and the local police, most of whom are conversant with English swear word vocabulary, closed down his premises. He renamed it Ace in the Hole which actually isn't totally devoid of ambiguity either.

Some of the Thai proprietors of the 1970s were sophisticated marketing gurus. One of the earliest night clubs in Walking Street, then as now the centre of the action, was called Tiffany's - not to be confused with a transvestite show at the other end of town.

This particular pleasure haven at the time provided attractive hostesses and female go-go dancers on stage until the stroke of midnight when there was an abrupt change of mood. The young women were replaced by young men in underpants or posing pouches on the brightly-lit catwalk. The straight tourists then left, apart from the overtly curious, and their places were taken by gay ones. This particular model of gay and straight integration was not followed up by later generations of club owners and remains unique to this day in Thailand and perhaps throughout the world.

Incidentally, that particular Tiffany's closed many years ago allegedly following one of those mysterious fires which tend to happen at dawn shortly after the insurance premium has been renewed.

By the mid 1970s Pattaya had reached a peak. But the Americans were leaving to lick their wounds at home. Was Pattaya's future to be bright or bleak? The answer was already blowing in the wind. Pattaya was determined to prove it could survive come what may.

TWO: BOOMS AND SLUMPS

The earliest predictions about Pattaya's future following the withdrawal of American forces from south east Asia were wildly inaccurate. But nobody at first seemed able to think of a strategy for the resort now that the bottom had fallen out of its role as provider of rest and recreation for the American military.

A British tour guide of the mid-1970s claimed "We suggest you omit Pattaya from your itinerary in Thailand as we understand that many commercial premises and places of entertainment have closed or will do so in the near future."

That was, of course, totally wrong. But it should be noted en passant that the resort's eclipse has been wrongly proclaimed on many other occasions too. The publicity surrounding hiv/aids as early as the early 1990s led to predictions that the days of prostitution would be numbered. "The sun and sex resort of Pattaya can hardly survive the frightening revelation that unprotected sex can lead to an unpleasant death," screamed a British tabloid newspaper which has since closed down.

Other soothsayers have thought that the Asian and bird flu pandemics, the Asian economic crisis of 1997, the Thai military coups in 1991 and 2006 and the Bangkok street riots in 2010 would lead to tourists abandoning Pattaya or even Thailand as a whole. But Pattaya has shown again and again that it is very adaptable and ever-changing. Indeed, by 2012, the Pattaya City Hall authorities were proclaiming that the best was yet to come and that the resort would be the Thai equivalent of the French Riviera within the next 10 years.

The end of the American imperialist dream in south east Asia led to other nationalities taking over. During the 1980s the British and the Germans established their own enclaves in south and north Pattaya respectively which, to some extent, have survived to this day. For many years the British provided more male tourists and expats than any other nationality in Pattaya.

British-owned bars and businesses sprang up to cater for the annual rush of vacationers. Bangers and mash and fish and chips were dutifully provided for UK tourists who were in reality seeking a tropical Manchester but with a hot sun, cheap beer and on-demand sex.

These British small-business entrepreneurs, who usually married Thai women in order to reduce the danger of being arrested by the immigration authorities, can still be found in the resort today. Some sociologists argue these pioneers are the consequence of Britain's post-imperial blues. That theory means that Britain has lost its world empire and no longer needs armies and bureaucrats to run the various countries under its control. As a result, the travel-loving Brits turn to starting small businesses in exotic locations as an alternative way to see the world and to leave behind the cold and dreary UK. It's an overblown theory, but there's maybe a grain of truth in it. A survey in a British newspaper in 2012, admittedly at a time of deep recession in Europe, suggested that almost a half of the UK population would emigrate if they had the opportunity to do so. A fair number fancied opening a business in a tropical climate.

A typical example was Loong John, a lanky Scotsman who married a Thai lady and opened a humble cafeteria near Pattaya's Central Road in the 1980s. His menu was very limited and, on some nights, even restricted to mince and tatties or a peppery stew made from a secret recipe from the Highlands.

But Pattaya in those days was full of British holidaymakers on cheap package tours. Sensibly, Loong John bought a guitar and there were sing-songs to be heard on most evenings as customers swilled down their grub with a couple of Singha beers. There were several golden and income-generating years as songs such as Knees Up Mother Brown and Stop Yer Tickling Jock astonished the local motorbike taxi boys and the street food sellers. But Loong John's business sank when the age of the cheap British package tourist came to an end in the early 1990s. These packages became a burden to the tour operators as we shall see.

Thai immigration statistics and the British embassy in Bangkok both claim that around 850,000 British tourists currently come to Thailand every year. There was a nosedive in early 2014 because of the political trouble in Bangkok. Yet the figure has remained remarkably constant over the years and was only overtaken by the number of Russian visitors as late as 2012. But the numbers are certainly overstated because the Thai immigration authority counts every passport presented at a Thai airport or a border post as a "new" person. Consequently, there is considerable over-counting as many foreigners, both expats and long-term tourists, leave Thailand and return several times in the course of a year. As an example, I left Thailand briefly four times in 2012 and so count as four separate visitors. One guy, an extremely well-paid oil rig worker in the

Middle East, frequently visits Thailand for a long weekend. He counted as 12 "new" visitors.

None the less, the turnover of Brits is still immense even though much of the British media have always been dubious about Pattaya's charms. A consumer magazine of 1982 described the resort as one of the world's worst 10 destinations on account of its blatant sex industry and polluted sea water. In those days British travel agents were overwhelmed by single men, or those claiming to be so, demanding night-owl packages with three weeks for the price of two at hotels with liberal overnight-guest policies. The night-owl packages tended to fizzle out in the 1990s as they were too much trouble for the companies organizing them. If a Brit lost his passport, or was involved in a traffic accident, or slipped on the bathroom floor, or picked up a man thinking it was a woman, or needed urgent cash or whatever, the tour operator was saddled with the unwelcome responsibility of "doing" something. Better let the luckless traveller sort out his own problems. Or seek out the British embassy.

Indeed one of my first embassy cases occurred when the night receptionist and security guard in a cheap Pattaya hotel were knocked unconscious and the contents of every mini-safe in the main lobby forced open and emptied by thieves who then fled on motorbikes. This meant that more than 20 British visitors needed new passports, not to mention the fact that many of them were without cash or traveller's cheques.

The extremely harassed travel company representative, who wisely was staying at a much more elegant hotel, told me, "This is the straw that broke the camel's back. From now on we no longer do package tours to Sin City."

My own role was limited to handing out passport replacement forms, pointing out the location of the nearest photocopy shop and waving off everybody as they journeyed to Bangkok in two uncomfortable minibuses to use the embassy's public phones to contact their nearest and dearest back in UK. "I'm in real trouble," confessed one young man, "My mother thinks I'm in Paignton England, not Pattaya Thailand." He was one of many Brits who were anxious to hide from family, friends or employer where exactly they spend their holiday.

By the early 1990s Pattaya was booming again on the international stage and acquiring a distinctly cosmopolitan feel which is even more obvious today. As early as 1985 there was an Arab quarter in South Pattaya which then, as now, is renowned for its particularly loud music and soft drinks. The Australians, the Japanese and the South Koreans discovered that there were many excellent golf courses even if a tiny minority of the single males did leave their clubs at the airport shed to indulge in more earthy pursuits. Incidentally, it's true to say that tourism remained very largely a male preserve. I'm told, for instance, that no foreign female tourist died in Pattaya until 2004 even though hundreds of foreign men have expired here, usually as a result of heart attacks, liver disease or traffic accidents.

What changed the male dominance in Pattaya tourism was the arrival of the Russians. As early as 2000 many of the resort's hotels and restaurants were providing Russian language menus and real estate companies soon cottoned on to the notion as well. By 2012 whole areas of the city were Russian conclaves, especially in the Naklua area, and it's well known that Russian businessmen are now one of the major foreign players in purchasing condominiums in the resort. The main Pattaya cable TV providers now have a good selection of channels in Russian. Even Woody Woodpecker cartoons have been translated for television.

There is even a growing number of road signs in Russian, including an unusual one situated on Pratumnak Hill warning that the upcoming, blind and nasty bend in the road could be the last thing you'll ever see. In July 2013 an information and advice office, operated by Russians to help their fellow-nationals with legal and other problems, was opened in Jomtien. Interestingly this venture was apparently not supported visibly by the Russian embassy network in Thailand. It was more of a commercial venture I was told.

What is noticeable about the Russians is that that they often come as a family: husbands, wives and the kids. Much the same is true of the Ukraine and the "Stan" republics of the former Soviet Union. Babes in arms are a common sight in the immigration bureau these days as their parents dutifully extend their own visas (kids under 15 can overstay for free in Thailand). It is still too early properly to assess the impact of Russian visitors and businesses on Pattaya, but it's surely a huge one. There is also the point, in many British eyes at least, that the Russians have taken over from the Germans as those dastardly people who shout too much, grab all the best places round the hotel pool and hungrily decimate the breakfast buffet whilst you are still having a shower.

The most recent wave of foreign tourists is from China, the new land of the package traveller. Each morning Pattaya Beach Road is now choked with large tourist buses unloading their passengers by the hundred to take the short boat ride to the neighbouring island of Ko Larn. A recent survey in Beijing found that only one percent of the Chinese population had yet visited Thailand but that 50 percent wanted to come. Yet one foreign visitor to Thailand in every four is already a Chinese national. Nobody, apart from the executives of five star hotels, seems to worry about the carbon footprint in Pattaya arising from such growth and perhaps that is just as well. Some commentators believe that, within 20 years, China will be linked by hi-speed trains to all south east Asian countries. Slowly but surely Pattaya is becoming an Asian resort. The pace will quicken once the Asean Economic Community, a potential free-trade zone of ten regional countries, begins to come on stream at the start of 2016.

Nobody really knows how big Pattaya is today. The skyline is dotted with high-rise condominiums and the resort is said to contain almost a hundred estate agents. There are fewer than 200,000 Thais registered in the Pattaya and Jomtien areas, but that's because many more work here in the hospitality industry – and increasingly in the construction and engineering sectors – but retain their registration and voting rights in their home province.

Thailand as a whole is currently receiving around 24 million foreign visitors a year and it's a fair estimate that one third of them comes to Pattaya as part of the vacation. These estimated eight million arrivals per year in Pattaya are accompanied by a similar number of Thai domestic tourists. Pattaya City Hall has stated that the eastern seaboard could be welcoming double those numbers by the end of the decade.

Income from tourism in Pattaya could soon exceed a trillion baht annually. Already Pattaya has more Mercedes cars on its roads than any other city of comparable size in the world, mostly owned by rich Thai businessmen. Some of the latter are already contemplating the rich pickings to be harvested if Thailand should follow Singapore and allow licensed casinos.

The big debate right now amongst foreigners is whether Pattaya has really changed all that much or whether it's still basically a red light district. It's true that the resort still has well-established bar and nightclub districts, pre-eminently The Walking Street and Sexy Soi Six. Most of the many novels published about Pattaya also take the view that Pattaya is still a rip-off zone where foreign tourists are bled white one way and another by nubile Thais or by foreign crooks posing as pillars of the local community. The investigative journalist Andrew Drummond, who has specialized in revealing the scams by which foreign criminals rip off their fellow-countrymen, has rarely said a good word about Pattaya. Mind you, he lives in Bangkok. But he rarely says a good word about that either.

On the other hand, Pattaya has massively expanded in recent years, yet the sex industry hasn't really grown with it. For example, the three main gay districts, Boyztown, Sunee Plaza and the Jomtien Complex, are much less busy than they were 10 years ago. Much of Sunee Plaza is in fact up for rent and I don't mean rent boys. Boyztown in terms of customers is but a shadow of its former self and Jomtien Complex has long since lost its major following. The heterosexually-dominant Walking Street, truth to tell, is less busy than it used to be and the side alleys leading from the popular main thoroughfare are mostly quiet, even deserted on some evenings. Lots of tourists still amble through the most famous street in Pattaya but they don't spend the money on the scale they used to. Ask any club owner. The word around town is that the most profitable businesses these days in the tourist areas are the 24-hour convenience stores.

This is not to say that the sex industry is dead. Rather it has changed: customers and prostitutes now increasingly meet by the social media and by mobile phone. Still, business sex has probably declined relative to Pattaya's monumental growth. The city now equals Bangkok with its five star hotels, top-class shopping malls, huge condos, excellent restaurants, sports facilities and opportunities for family entertainment. Good quality schools and hospitals mean that Pattaya can support foreign families with the necessary infrastructure. Without it, foreigners just won't settle. Neighbouring districts such as Laem Chabang (the country's largest port facility), Amata City (an expanding industrial park with tax incentives provided by the government) and Map Ta Put (the world's eighth largest petrochemical hub) all employ many foreigners as managers.

In recent years Pattaya has been particularly well-served by its local executives. The respective previous and current mayors, Niran Wattanasartsathorn and Itthiphol Kunplume, have encouraged investment by both the public and private sectors and have developed the facilities to such an extent that Pattaya is now recognized as an international host centre for major sporting events and music festivals. Problems there certainly are: street crime, pollution and traffic snarl-ups to name but three. But the diversification of Pattaya in recent years and its evolution from a single-attraction entertainment zone to a relatively sophisticated international city is an amazing story. The change from fishing village to concrete jungle has even been achieved without as many of the electricity brownouts and water shortages which have plagued urban sprawl in many European and American cities.

None the less, readers may be relieved to learn that, in the following pages, this theme will not be followed up in detail. Being British honorary consul means dealing with the Brits and to that grim subject we next turn next.

In fact, the first British lager louts arrived in Thailand 400 years ago!

THREE: QUEEN VICTORIA'S STATUE

The British have been around in Thailand since the early 17th century when the first sailing ship arrived not too far from where Pattaya stands today, ostensibly for reasons of trade. But the vessel was heavily armed and the crew had been at sea for many months. The only entertainment they had seen in ages was one of their colleagues being flogged for falling asleep on watch.

Many of these early Brits were essentially pirates whose appetite for booze and sex outsized anything their tourist descendants have managed to achieve in our own times. The situation was so serious that by the 19th century the Thais became truly concerned that they might actually be colonized by Britain especially after a particularly successful military campaign by the British army in nearby Burma in 1826.

But no. Thailand remains the only country in south east Asia to escape having been conquered if we forget the half-example of the Japanese in Bangkok during the Second World War. But the Thais managed to avoid being swallowed up by Britain or later by France, the main imperialist powers in the region, by a combination of clever diplomacy, some modernizing reforms and a hefty dose of good luck. In 1909 an Anglo-Siamese treaty fixed the borders between Thailand and Malaya which have remained controversial ever since. You can, if you wish, blame Britain for the violence still occurring in Thailand's three most southerly provinces.

In those far off days, British visitors to Thailand could do pretty much as they pleased. They could be tried for offences only in British consular courts, which met very rarely if at all, and could even seek legal protection through their Thai lovers and wives. In 1797 a British seaman was allowed to escape Scot-free from a charge of raping 35 Thai women because his (obviously hired) wife claimed she was perfectly capable of satisfying him alone and without mass help. This discriminatory situation began to change slowly only after the military coup of 1932 which saw the collapse of the absolute monarchy and Thailand's halting progress towards some sort of democracy with at least some rules and regulations. The king at that time abdicated three years later and retired with his queen to Surrey in southern England. He was the only Thai king ever to abdicate and died in 1941. His adopted son fought in the Battle of Britain against Hitler's air force.

Diplomatically, the original British legation to Thailand was built on the banks of the Chao Phraya river in the 19th century although the precise date is uncertain. It is well-nigh impossible to find out now what the legation actually did, if anything, as most material on the internet under the heading History of the British Embassy in Bangkok is devoted to angry British subjects from our own day complaining about the dreadful embassy services, run by incompetents and time-servers, and moaning about the woeful unfairness of the visa system for Thai ladies trying to get into Britain to be re-united with their boyfriends. "Thanks for nothing," writes one Brit from Sheffield whose girlfriend has been rebuffed for the fifth time.

In the 1920s the current site in Wireless Road, then a remote and charming rural spot, was built by a British architect although the actual step of being upgraded to full embassy status was delayed until 1947. At more than 13 acres, it was always too big for comfort and the noisiest and dirtiest three acres, overlooking the polluted Ploenchit Road, were sold off to a private developer in 2006 for a reported 50 million pounds to build a shopping centre. At the time there was much fuss in the British press about Whitehall miserliness and greed taking pride of place over Empire (whatever that meant), but in reality the site needed trimming down. The volume of work simply didn't require all that space.

The main problem was what to do with Queen Victoria. Her black statue had been moved from the old legation in 1926 to the Wireless Road site and, during World War Two, she was boarded up. However the Japanese occupiers did provide a peephole so that the old queen would not feel too upset. In 2006 it was realized that Victoria would now be facing a blank wall waiting for the new developer to build a shopping centre and she was moved to a quieter spot near the ambassador's residence which was unaffected by the land sale. Victoria's statue has always been popular with local Thai women who believe that she had, and still retains, the psychic ability to award them the winning lottery numbers or the symbolic authority to give them many children. After all, Victoria did have many offspring of her own although there is no record of her winning the lottery. Or even buying a ticket come to that.

Like most British citizens finding themselves in Thailand for whatever reason, I had never been inside the embassy's hallowed territory in Wireless Road. I had a vague idea that if you had a serious problem in Thailand the embassy might offer you a cup of tea and do what was necessary to bail you out – a naïve view indeed but one which is still remarkably common today – but beyond that my mind was a blank. How I first came across the British embassy is probably unique in the annals of diplomacy.

In 1994 I opened Pattaya bridge club with an Australian friend. Playing cards is a rather sensitive subject in Thailand although it's the gambling which is illegal and not the actual playing of the game. Although we went to extraordinary lengths to license the club and to affiliate it to the contract bridge association of Thailand, there were suspicions at the local police station that we might be up to no good, especially as we were foreigners. Located in a local restaurant in the city centre, one afternoon we underwent a formal raid from a police major, 12 accompanying officers and two Black Marias as somebody had reported that there was money being displayed on the tables. Eventually we managed to convince the police major that the money was there to pay for teas and coffees and had nothing to do with gambling. But it was a close-run thing. I sold the club for a sillily low fee in 2001 but it still exists successfully today and has its own website. I recently rejoined and am happy to report that the standard of bidding and of play has improved markedly over the past twenty years.

Sadly, at Christmas 1996, one of the elderly male members had a sudden heart attack at the club and promptly died holding a very powerful hand of 25 high-card points (for the bridge players amongst you). Stefan was originally a Ukrainian guy who had become a naturalised British citizen after World War Two and had eventually retired in Thailand. He claimed to have been at Auschwitz although whether as a guard or as a prisoner was hotly debated at the time and still is. The restaurant staff immediately called the local police and the body-bag volunteers. Stefan was taken to the main government-run mortuary in Bangkok for the inevitable autopsy.

Somebody suggested that I, as the person vaguely in charge of the bridge club, should notify the British embassy in Bangkok which proved impossible. Nobody answered the phone after four o'clock and, during the Christmas recess, perhaps not at all. These days, emergencies of that sort can be handled more professionally (I hope) by the British Foreign Office's international crisis call centre, but in 1996 all you received was a recorded voice telling you not to bother until the next day, assuming it wasn't a weekend or a public holiday. I also spent the entire evening at Pattaya police station unable to answer any of the questions fired at me about Stefan's lifestyle, general health, family and next of kin. One of the investigators persistently thought a bridge club was for the benefit of construction industry workers. "You need a work permit here to build bridges," cautioned the senior cop, "it's not like in England you know."

The next morning my phone call to the Bangkok embassy was put through to the consular section where a very charming female voice informed me that they didn't have a representative in Pattaya at the moment but that they wished me all the best in sorting out any problems concerning the death. Fortunately, the embassy did have on record Stefan's Pattaya address and, armed with this vital information, I paid a visit to his humble town house in the company of two policemen. Access to the residence was difficult as Stefan's two barking dogs were very hungry and angry by this time, but we managed to assuage them after a local food stall provided the necessary skin and bones at a discounted rate in view of the sad circumstances. A neighbor told us he had lived alone but liked young Thai females of which there had been a constant procession through his front door.

During a search of the house, I also discovered that Stefan's nearest relative, a sister, lived in England and the embassy quickly contacted her to break the bad news. Unfortunately they had not spoken to each other for several years and she refused to have anything to do with the funeral arrangements or to offer any cash to offset expenses. "I know what he was doing in Thailand," she said sourly and I got the impression she didn't mean bridge.

Eventually I managed to arrange a local cremation with the financial help of some sympathetic bridge club members and even found a new home for the dogs. Stefan's meager possessions, comfortably packed into two single suitcases, were handed on to a local charity after the UK-based sister said she was not interested.

Some weeks later, in early 1997, I received a phone call from the consular section of the Bangkok embassy asking if I could pay them a visit to sign some paperwork arising from Stefan's case. The embassy was huge in those days and it was eight years before the sale of part of the site to build a shopping centre. I paid my brief respects to Queen Victoria and a war memorial before being escorted to the office of the then consul Brian Kelly. He was a kindly man nearing retirement and a person of few words it appeared. Without referring the deceased Stefan, he asked if I would be interested in acting as a consular correspondent in Pattaya for the British embassy. It was an unpaid post, he explained, but shouldn't take up a lot of time as Pattaya was really quite a small place. However, he added, necessarily incurred travel and phone costs could be reimbursed. Overwhelmed by this expression of confidence in a complete stranger, I agreed. My formal interview had lasted all of five minutes.

As I returned to Pattaya on the express bus – the expenses did not run to a taxi – I began to wonder what exactly I had agreed to. I had been told by Brian's deputy that the part-time post involved writing a report on British deaths in the resort, visiting prisons from time to time and occasionally going to see the seriously sick in hospital. As regards training, there were apparently regional courses held from time to time but the next one would not be organized for several months and would take place in Kuala Lumpur in Malaysia. "Until then, old boy," I was told, "the best of British and always remember we are here to help." But only between 8.30 am and 4.00 pm, I was reminded, and excluding weekends and public holidays.

But what exactly was a consular correspondent? When I got home I couldn't wait to look up the term on the internet. The response there was most alarming. Of course, these were early days for that particular form of new technology. The first reference was to a secret agent of the British government who had been shot dead in Papua New Guinea whilst filming a camp site at night. The second concerned a volunteer in India who had been trapped for two days when a riot broke out in the prison where he was visiting a forlorn Brit who couldn't afford the air ticket back to London. The third concerned an embassy volunteer who was kidnapped whilst claiming to be photographing birds at an airfield in remote Pakistan.

It was beginning to look as if I had bitten off more than I could chew.

FOUR: BRITS IN THE SHITS

I soon discovered that the British embassy in Bangkok was a complex creature. In 1997 it was the largest embassy in Asia and second in size world-wide only to the one in Washington DC. The Bangkok mission was divided into several sections with a total staff of around one hundred and fifty. There was the political section which handled Anglo-Thai relations, housed the press department and kept the ambassador briefed on sensitive issues. The visa section controlled visas for Thais (and also for Laos citizens) trying to visit the UK, whilst the business section encouraged investment in both Thailand and UK. Incidentally, my sole contribution to industry and trade during my term of office with the embassy was to introduce a British entrepreneur who wanted to manufacture potato crisps in the Land of Smiles. I may be the only British consular official ever to have received through the post as a Christmas present a dozen packs of "Salt n' Vinegar".

The department to which I was attached was the consular section which, broadly speaking, handled welfare including the issuing of British passports, providing notarial services and coming to the assistance of Brits in trouble. It was led by a consul or first secretary, always a British career diplomat, and had a full time staff of around twenty, the majority being locally employed Thais. The native Brits were an ever-changing bunch, typically returning to the UK or being transferred after three years, and it became clear that the Thais, although mostly inferior in rank, actually ran the embassy de facto and were the main point of continuity for the day-to-day bureaucracy.

The embassy octopus was centred on Bangkok and its tentacles in the Thai provinces were weak in those days. But there was an honorary British consulate (an actual office) in Chiang Mai which was a point of contact for the expat Brits and visitors there as well as providing some written services such as letters of income for applicants for one year visas at Thai immigration and marriage registration documentation. The Chiang Mai consulate survives to this day and has been largely immune from the cuts and downsizing which have been the hallmark of the British government abroad in recent years. There was also an honorary consul in Phuket but he was a stand-alone figure, without a formal office or back-up, whose greatest moment of triumph lay in team-leading the British response to the 2004 Boxing Day tsunami, the third largest earthquake ever recorded.

I realized soon enough that the embassy's experience of its Pattaya representation had been a troubled one. One honorary consul had agreed to meet with investigative journalists from the Sunday UK press and had been quietly dismissed after details of his alleged private life appeared in a sensational tabloid exposure.

At least two other consular correspondents – the higher position of honorary consul had been dropped in the meantime as far as Pattaya was concerned – gave up the position in quick succession as they did not want to be bothered with what one of them called "riff-raff knocking on my door asking for money".

This was his personal summary of the quality of British tourists to Pattaya. This particular man, an expat hotel manager, was quietly dismissed after suggesting that a holidaymaker from Sheffield who had been robbed in a bar should "sod off" as it was after midnight when he phoned, or attempted to anyway.

The position of consular correspondent in Pattaya had been vacant for some months when I assumed the diplomatic, lowly office in 1997. In those days the embassy did not routinely use the internet or email and the sole method of communicating with the main site was by phone or fax. Initial advice from superiors had been thin on the ground, to say the least, but I had been warned to expect more or less anything and not to take any major decisions without consulting the main site consular section, preferably by fax.

"By all means listen to people's problems, but don't believe much of what you hear," was the succinct advice of one female colleague in Bangkok. She added that I shouldn't worry if I decided to resign after a few months as that was par for the course in Pattaya. "They don't last long you know," adding "actually it's a bit of a nightmare down there as Pattaya has eaten alive several of your predecessors." I had to hope I was made of sterner stuff.

As events turned out, my first case was almost my last. Mrs Young was a Thai lady who had married a British guy who had then suddenly died, leaving his penniless wife to bring up their three year daughter Lena in the Pattaya area. I received a phone call from the embassy asking me to phone Mrs Young and make an appointment to see her as she believed she might be entitled to some financial benefit from the British government. "Handing out money is an unpopular subject in the foreign office in London, so try not to say too much," was the guarded advice from the vice-consul of the day. I persistently rang the phone number given to me but neither Mrs Young nor anybody else picked up the phone. Baffled, I paid a visit to the local telecommunications office in Pattaya – an early example of using your initiative I suppose – and managed to find out that the number had been disconnected because of non-payment of the bill.

Whilst I was pondering what to do next, if anything, I happened by chance to glance at a local newspaper to see the sprawling and alarming headline "British embassy leaves family to starve in Pattaya". There followed a heart-breaking tale of Mrs Young having to beg in the streets for food to keep her young daughter alive. Still, I reasoned, the newspaper must know how to contact Mrs Young. Thus my next port of call was the newspaper office where I introduced myself and said I would try to help. The newspaper editor gladly, perhaps too gladly, offered to fix up a meeting which was scheduled for the next day. He said he had another "secret" phone number for Mrs Young which had not yet been disconnected.

My meeting with Mrs Young and Lena took place in the street adjacent to the newspaper office and I was astonished to see they were accompanied by a large Thai TV crew representing several local channels, both Thai and English speaking. It was a set-up! I was pressed by reporters in two languages to say what exactly the British government or the embassy could do to prevent the bereft family from starving. This was a difficult question indeed as my knowledge of UK pensions for overseas widows and children was precisely zero. However, I promised to contact my superiors and get hold of the necessary forms and leaflets. But I did have the presence of mind to suggest that the newspaper start a cash fund to assist Mrs Young and Lena in their distress in the meantime. That night I was the top story on local cable TV.

The embassy top-brass was not exactly ecstatic to discover that my first assignment had led to substantial and unwelcome coverage in the local media on a technical subject which was sensitive by any stretch of imagination and about which I knew nothing whatsoever.

"This really isn't cricket you know," commented one consular official in Bangkok whilst immediately admitting that he didn't know much about overseas pensions for the widows of dead Brits either. "You have to play a low profile," he added whilst not clarifying what to do when confronted by a team of newsmen with cameras and microphones pointing in your direction.

However, the whole matter blew over. In due course I was sent a packet crammed with forms written in bureaucratic English to be completed by benefit claimants. As Mrs Young didn't read bureaucratic English, or any other sort come to that, I filled in the forms on her behalf, risking instant dismissal for impersonating someone. However, some months later, Mrs Young received from the British government a modest widow's overseas pension which was permanently frozen and not subject to inflation increases. Incidentally, this automatic financial loophole for foreign widows of British nationals was cancelled, or at any rate curtailed, by the UK government as recently as 2013 as a cash-saving exercise.

Most of them receive only a one-off death grant. Meanwhile the ongoing public campaign to raise money for the family in Pattaya was remarkably successful and some small cheques were even sent to Mrs Young via the embassy. Mrs Young and her now grown-up daughter remain friendly to this day. I began to appreciate the scale of the Foreign Office's responsibilities for

Brits worldwide. It's a truly enormous enterprise with perhaps one percent of all British travellers abroad seeking some kind of help. By 2012, according to the government's annual report British Behaviour Abroad, Thailand was ranked as the second most likely country after the Philippines where the percentage of British nationals needing consular assistance was to be found. In true diplomatic form, this statement is actually meaningless in context as far fewer Brits visit Manila than they do Bangkok. The report also indicated that British nationals were most likely to be hospitalized in Greece, followed by Thailand, and most prone to be detained by the police in Spain, followed by the USA and then Thailand. The real point is that Thailand usually figures somewhere in the top 10 countries when it comes to misery.

I learned too a great deal about what can happen to Brits abroad. Hospital patients who couldn't afford the costs, mentally-ill people who couldn't pay for their medication, Brits convicted of drugs offences and even sentenced to death, victims of street crimes of all descriptions, terrible motorbike crashes, murdered Brits and murdering Brits, lost and stolen passports, Brits running out of money, men whose lives were ruined after a foolish sexual escapade. All these and many more categories occupied much of my life for the next dozen years. I reckon during that time that I met, once or on an ongoing basis, at least 10,000 Brits in Pattaya who requested some sort of assistance, trivial or substantial. For many of my consular cases, or perhaps casualties is a more appropriate word, one visit to the Land of Smiles was enough for them.

Sometimes it was all just impossible. Under Foreign Office rules the embassy never pays bills, can't spring anybody from jail, doesn't give loans, can't find you a job, can't intervene with your bank or government department and doesn't offer legal advice. These, of course, were the most common requests made by often desperate and stranded people. What the embassy could and still can do is to listen, make people aware of their situation, contact friends and relatives overseas or in Thailand for financial assistance, visit those in prison or seriously hospitalized, suggest the names of local lawyers (without actually recommending them) and give procedural help to the next of kin if death strikes.

Some of the requests made for help were certainly odd. One London couple who were thinking of retiring to Thailand said they had heard that it was very easy to make mistakes over here and wanted to have an urgent meeting with me so that they wouldn't make any. They even brought along a tape-recorder. A university professor from Sheffield had heard there are a lot of prostitutes in Pattaya and wished to know the name and location of any bar where the girls were "genuine" and "not on the game". An ex-military man from Manchester approached me to find out what documents he would need to import a machine gun into Thailand, adding that he would bring over the bullets later if successful in the initial application.

The list was endless. A closet-transvestite from Brighton wanted to know if he would be attacked or arrested if he went out at night with a fur coat and in high heels. A pensioner from Bolton wanted a good tattooist to print a message on his chest not to cremate him as he was fearful he might wake up prematurely on the mortuary slab. One elderly lady from Redhill phoned me from her hotel room in Pattaya to explain she had run out of Pampers and was literally marooned.

I even suffered physical violence on occasion. The most serious incident was a curious matter which became known locally as The Meat and Two Veg Case. I had been telephoned by the embassy to try and locate a certain club in Pattaya's Sexy Soi Six which was named The 69 Experience or something very similar. The problem was that the British owner had a sister in Coventry who had recently died of a sudden heart attack. Foreign office protocol required me to tell the guy to phone his brother-in-law in UK for urgent information about a family matter. I was not allowed to say what the gruesome detail was just in case the whole thing was some kind of hoax. That had happened more than once in the past, especially on April 1 anniversaries.

The inside of the 69 Experience resembled a very downmarket version of the Kit Kat club in the movie Cabaret. However, all was silent and there was no sign of music or entertainment at the time of my arrival. This was because one of the staff, who had recently been dismissed for stealing, had smashed the sound system and destroyed the bar area before departing in a huff. I managed to locate the Brit owner with the dead sister and handed to him the appropriate relative's phone number in Coventry. Refusing the offer of a free drink amid the carnage, I noticed there appeared to be a back exit which might offer an escape route without fuss.

That was my mistake. The back exit led to a sort of dark alley where I was immediately surrounded by three large and tough-looking Thai transvestites without any trace of a smile on their faces. One of the trio was wearing a leather front and boots and the other two were also dressed to kill if you will pardon the expression. I learned later that the Pattaya slang in some quarters for cross-dressing thieves without scruples was Meat and Two Veg. None of them spoke a word, but the gang leader held out his hand in a gesture clearly designed to illustrate that they were the Dick Turpins and I was the luckless coach passenger.

Probably foolishly, I wasn't inclined to give up without a struggle in the course of which I suffered a couple of scratches, a pair of broken glasses and the loss of a wallet mercifully containing less than 10 pounds equivalent. Staggering to the nearby Beach Road, I was soon at the police station where I made the obligatory report when you are mugged.

This was the only occasion on which I as a consular officer had to make a report that I had been the victim of a crime. In the end, three policemen then obligingly returned with me to the back alley where the Meat and Two Veg trio were foolishly still lurking in the darkness, no doubt waiting for the next victim. They were frog-marched in handcuffs back to police headquarters where I decided it was simply not worth my time pressing charges, having to visit the court at least twice and doubtless appearing in controversial circumstances yet again on the local TV to the chagrin of my bosses. My wallet was still missing but one of the trio had a receipt from a very recent visit to a foreign exchange booth. Each Meat and Two Veg was fined 100 baht (about two pounds) before disappearing into the black night. The gender-bender in the leather outfit blew me a kiss as she left. It then occurred to me that they paid the fines with the money stolen from my wallet.

Such is life.

FIVE: THE GRIM REAPER

Although Pattaya is usually promoted as a good times destination, the Grim Reaper with his scythe is never long out of view. Neither the Thai government nor the local authorities publish statistics about the number of deaths, alien or Thai, so it's a bit of a guessing game. However, we do know from British embassy figures that several hundred Brits die in Thailand every year. That means an average of two or three Brits a week die in Pattaya alone.

The majority of the British deceased are elderly men, often retirees, with potentially fatal conditions such as cancer or hypertension-related illnesses. Deaths commonly occur in hospitals and the bursar is usually quick off-the-mark notifying the embassy, particularly where there is an outstanding bill for the nearest and dearest to pay. Autopsies on foreigners are a Thai police discretion, but will always be required unless there is a record of recent hospitalization and clear treatment immediately prior to the demise.

The most common reason for death in younger guys is to be involved in a road accident, usually driving a motorbike. Given that 30 Thai nationals die every day on average in road accidents, it's not surprising that there is a spill-over effect on the more adventuresome tourists. Thai motorbikes tend to have bigger engines than British ones and, given the poor standard of driving on often poorly-repaired roads, lethal accidents are commonplace.

To make matters worse, local insurance is not deemed compulsory for motorbike drivers or riders. Even when insurance is provided, the financial cover limits are much lower than normal in Europe. Some farangs in Thailand have ended up forking out their life savings to pay for lawyers' fees when defending themselves against causing a death by dangerous driving.

Pattaya has acquired a reputation in popular mythology for hosting an unusual number of suicides, especially jumps from the upper floors of condominiums. More than one curious journalist has attempted to get to the bottom of this matter. Is it something they put in the water? Is it connected with the fact that safety rails on Thai condo balconies tend to be on the low side? Are some of these so-called suicides actually murders in disguise? Actually the highest number of apparent suicides I dealt with during my time with the embassy was four in one year. But tap water, safety rails and murder most foul didn't appear in any of them. In fact, most of the tragedies were accidents related to larking-about on the balconies during a drinking session.

The truth of the matter is that suicides are newsworthy precisely because they are unusual. In these days of the social media, people like to read the gory details and gawp at the photos on the internet.

Sociologists use the term "deviancy amplification", or putting a social problem under the spotlight, to explain that the publicity generated leads to yet more media exposure, thus exaggerating the whole subject in ever-expanding circles. A good example occurred in 2009 when bloggers on a Pattaya-based internet site proclaimed that a British man had been found hanging upside down on a local pier with several wounds in the head and an ice-pick sticking in his ear. According to the site, local police had deemed it to be a suicide. Of course, they had done no such thing and the details given were very wide of the mark. But the tale was one of a series at the time designed to show that Pattaya was the world centre for unhappy Brits wanting to top themselves, each story furthering the idea that suicides are a Pattaya specialty.

None the less, a strong stomach is sometimes required. I was called by the local police one afternoon to a flat in central Pattaya where a neighbour had discovered the body of a British man lying on his bed with a plastic bag over his head and his wrists handcuffed to a rail which formed part of the steel bed head. Once the plastic bag was removed, the ghastly expression on his face with his eyes almost out of their sockets revealed a terrible death agony. As always, local TV crews accompanied the police to the scene of the crime of the spectacle and the gory tale hit the local news with the suggestion that the guy had been brutally murdered. After all how can you smother yourself with a plastic bag whilst your hands are pinioned? That's ridiculous eh?

The reality is that you can indeed take your own life in this way. The guy in question had drunk almost a whole bottle of cheap whisky before placing the bag over his head as the subsequent autopsy revealed. He had already prepared the handcuffs and quickly snapped them shut on the steel bed rail as his last mortal decision.

The fact that he was an alleged serial pedophile who was currently on bail for offences against young boys in Pattaya lent weight to this interpretation especially as he had left a scrawled suicide note, "I can't take any more". The British Sunday papers picked up on the story and one outlet printed the headline, "Pattaya pedophile murdered by moral crusaders". Nonsense actually! What he couldn't face was a long jail sentence in a Thai prison.

Although honorary consuls don't routinely investigate deaths, local police sought my informal help on many occasions. From the 15th floor of a Pattaya condominium a British man had jumped at dead of night and spattered himself all over the car park. Initially it did look like an accidental death. The condo balcony had a particularly low rail and there was the almost inevitable bottle of spirits nearby. Correspondence in his room showed that he had recently obtained a lecturing job in a Thai university to start three months later. The condominium staff confirmed the guy in question had many friends and had not shown signs of mental instability so far as they could ascertain.

Of course, an outside security camera might have been useful but it was not in operation at the time as a security guard regrettably had hung his jacket over the appliance whilst he had a tea break and had forgotten to collect it. But there were a couple of odd factors. In his suitcase there was a return air ticket to Manchester the very next day. This aroused my suspicions as it's a well-attested fact that wannabe-suicides on vacation often make the attempt just before they are due to fly back to serious problems at home. If this was accidental death, it was surely bad luck for it happen just hours before the return flight.

The other factor worth attention was that near to the almost-empty whisky bottle there was a small card propping up an empty glass. It was a membership card for a Manchester casino and, in due course, it was discovered that the guy had an outstanding gambling debt of around thirty thousand pounds. At his home address in UK, according to police, there was a whole pile of official-looking letters demanding urgent repayment as well as final-warning notices from Barclaycard and Mastercard threatening legal proceedings. Later his Manchester doctor told the inquest in UK that his patient had a record of attempted suicide. The dead can't speak, of course, but the inquest decided on a verdict of suicide. Most likely that was correct. Things aren't always what they initially seem to be.

Identifying dead bodies can be a nightmare. I accompanied forensic police officers to a wood on the outskirts of Pattaya where a male corpse, or what was left of it, was lying face down in a thicket. He was white-skinned and had been dead about three weeks. Car tracks nearby suggested he had perhaps been murdered elsewhere before being dumped in a secluded spot. Clearly the cause of death was a gunshot to the chest. He was wearing a green T-shirt and a pair of brown trousers. But who was he and what nationality was he?

Back at the local mortuary it was discovered that there was nothing in his pockets. However his underpants revealed a Marks and Spencer label, not definitive proof he was British but a small push in that direction and enough to spark my interest in his home-country. His brown shoes were very muddy but appeared to be heavier and to be more built-up than any commercial brand I had ever seen. After spraying the shoes with a hose, it became apparent that they had been specially made for him. It was just possible to make out the maker's name on the tongue of one shoe and a little detective work in UK produced the full address of the company and the identity of the murdered man. He had indeed suffered from a deformed foot. Later Thai police inquiries suggested he had been a drugs-mule who had tried to cheat the Thai mafia. That's a mistake you make only once in the Land of Smiles.

Shortly before I retired from the embassy, I checked through my records and saw that I had had some involvement in following up on the deaths of over 1,000 Brits in the Pattaya area. More than three quarters were straightforward cases of older guys dying from lifestyle diseases, typically heart attacks, and of younger men acting rashly on motorbikes. There wasn't much one could do except to be sympathetic towards the relatives, inform them of procedures such as death certificates, put them in contact with morticians and remind them, if need be, that the embassy never ever pays any bills. Dead or alive!

Yet that leaves around 200 cases of sudden death in Pattaya not so easy to explain. Behind the suicides lay a great deal of human misery: men (hardly any women) who were suffering from a terminal disease, had lost the will to carry on, had run out of cash, were betrayed in love or business or were facing police investigations in Thailand or abroad. Accidental deaths in my experience were often fuelled by alcohol or drugs. I recall the very respectable parents of a 23 year old Brit from Portsmouth who could not bring themselves to believe that their son was a heroin addict even though the needle was still in his arm in a room locked and bolted from the inside and without an alternative access point. He had died of overdosing with the low-grade bad stuff he had foolishly bought on the street.

Sometimes it was impossible to tell what had happened. A middle-aged British teacher working at an independent school in Pattaya drowned whilst taking a customary midnight swim in Pattaya bay. By the time the police had tracked down his identity and local address two days later, his Thai girlfriend had emptied their flat of all valuables, had raided his bank account and had disappeared. The autopsy did not reveal any additional information. Did he have a sudden cramp attack or was he murdered? Back in the UK, the coroner's court demanded comprehensive details from the Thai police, but the only available documentation was a brief account by the policeman called to the beach and a single paragraph autopsy report. No serious attempt was ever made to find the Thai girlfriend. Regrettably there are very few lieutenant Columbos in the Thai police force asking "just one more thing". The British coroner recorded an open verdict.

Murders of foreigners in Pattaya, and Thailand generally, are mercifully on the rare side and are usually ordered by Thais who are aggrieved or feel they have seriously lost face. A number of British men have got mixed up with selling drugs, usually to try and make sorely needed extra cash, but failed to pay their Thai masters their due. They should have remembered that a contract killing in Thailand starts with a fee as low as one thousand pounds. Life can indeed be very cheap indeed in Sin City. I recall a Brit from Liverpool who battered his Thai wife half-to-death in a drunken stupor and was repaid by her relatives by being cut up and deposited in various plastic bin-liners round the city.

Death on occasion also produces its own kind of gallows-humour. A headless corpse was found by fishermen floating in Pattaya bay. Although the torso had become decomposed and had been half-eaten by sea creatures, the remains clearly showed it was male, white and (judging from the skin) belonged to someone in his late 50s or 60s. The identity remained a total mystery until, joy of joys, another group of fishermen found a head floating without a body attached to it in the same coastal area. Police cars with sirens screeching raced to the coastal road. But expectation turned to disappointment when it was discovered that the head belonged to a black guy in his early 20s. Neither case was ever solved.

Certainly the oddest question I have ever been asked about death came from a wife from Accrington, Lancashire, whose elderly husband had died of alcoholic poisoning and lung cancer in Pattaya. She had arrived to take back the body to the United Kingdom to be buried in the family vault, or so she said. The lady was not particularly upset by the demise of her spouse as she explained in frank detail that he had not had an erection for some years.

However, she did express surprise that the gin had helped to kill him because he was ultra-careful always to take it with fresh orange juice which, as we all know, is good for your health.

Her astonishment seemed to be that the good didn't cancel out the poisonous.

The lady from Accrington had many questions to ask about transporting bodies back to UK and seemed reluctant to leave the matter in the hands of the very competent international funeral directors available in Thailand. She wanted to know details such as whether the lead-lined coffin used to transport the dead on scheduled airlines was reusable and what exactly mummifying and fluid draining meant at the level of detail. She also wanted to find out whether passengers on a flight could object to a corpse being carried in the hold, assuming that is that they found out in time. Usually coffins are loaded onto planes long before the travelling public reaches the tarmac.

But her final question was the ultimate in more senses than one.

"Do you think," she enquired with a frown, "that it would be OK if I placed a carrier bag in the coffin?" When I asked what would be in the afore-mentioned bag, she explained, "It's for his duty free goods you see!"

This was likely the only time in recorded history that a request was made for a corpse to proceed through immigration control with 200 cigarettes and a bottle of spirits. They were, of course, the very items which had been responsible for his death in the first place.

SIX: THAT'S YOUR FUNERAL

When the ultimate tragedy strikes abroad, it's natural for the surviving family and friends to look for the familiar in a time of stress. So when someone dies in Thailand, it's likely that those left behind will assume that the procedures are similar to those appertaining back in the old country. Unfortunately, Thai cultural norms can be very different from British leading to upsets which can enforce rather than diminish a family tragedy.

Assuming the local police require an autopsy to be performed – which they do routinely for foreigners unless an obviously sick person spent his last days in hospital – the body will be taken quickly to the police autopsy unit in Bangkok. I recall vividly a devout Jehovah's Witness whose son had died in a vehicle pile-up in Pattaya. Dad took the next flight to Thailand and moved heaven and earth to oppose an autopsy on religious grounds which he claimed were more important than life itself. He even sent an impassioned letter to the British ambassador. But all to no avail and the autopsy did show that the young man was drunk at the time of the accident. This revelation in turn invalidated the medical insurance – the victim had not shown "reasonable care" – and the family had to pay around eight thousand pounds for refrigerated accommodation, the autopsy itself and the return journey of the corpse to Carlisle in northern England. Don't drink and drive takes on a new meaning when you're on holiday in Thailand.

In most cases the embassy does remarkably little. It is an official duty to ascertain the next of kin, no matter where located in the world, so that a "letter of release" can be issued which permits the body to be moved to a Thai crematorium or be prepared for the air journey for repatriation. Sometimes it is far from easy to find out the identity or location of the nearest and dearest. A 45 year old Brit died of a sudden heart attack in a Pattaya hotel. He was unmarried and had no children. The nearest relative was a father who was known to be in Australia but without a specific location known. The British High Commission in Canberra did their best, but the older guy still had not surfaced after four months. The bill for refrigeration was climbing at around twenty pounds a day and the British embassy, you recall, won't pay such expenses. Eventually, the Thai mortuary authorities took unilateral action and buried him at a hillside graveyard near Pattaya where Thais and foreigners without anyone to bear the costs sometimes end up with or without an accompanying coffin.

It is actually a myth that Buddhist countries never resort to interment. But these cemeteries are places of enormous superstition in traditional Thai culture and sightings of earth-bound ghosts and discovery of non-corrupt bodies in graveyards are legion as the skeletons are routinely dug up and burned in a religious rite after a few years in order to make way for new arrivals. Three months after this particular interment, the angry father turned up in Pattaya asking what had happened to his son. He demanded an exhumation and tried to sue the mortuary and local authority officials involved who had disposed of his heir without permission. After spending a fortune with local lawyers, he was forced to give up. Under Thai law there's nobody to sue in cases such as this. As the unpaid bills mount your rights disappear.

Thai autopsies do tend to be somewhat superficial affairs – the report is sometimes just one short paragraph as we have seen – so it is always open to the relatives or even the authorities at home to demand a second one in the UK. In 2003 a British businessman Robert Henry was discovered dead in a swamp in Jomtien. He had been shot several times in the head amid rumours of involvement by local mafia figures. The second autopsy in UK did indeed reveal some remarkable differences from the first in Bangkok and the suggested trajectories of the bullets were very different in the two accounts. These findings in turn led to a rethink about whether he had been shot in a car sat-down or whilst standing up and his body taken for dumping in the swamp. Later a suspected hitman Paul Cryne was acquitted at Pattaya court after several key witnesses failed to turn up. Mr Cryne appears later in this book in a wider but unusually horrific context.

About 90 percent of Brits who die in Thailand are cremated in the country. The final farewell takes place in a Thai temple with a gas-fired oven. Only in the most remote districts of northern Thailand do you find these days any open-air cremations on a burning pile of wood and coconut shells. The cost depends on the location of the temple and the amount of pomp and ritual required: the more the number of monks in attendance the greater the cost. Cremation prices have risen steeply in recent years and are now at least in excess of a thousand pounds and sometimes substantially more. Morticians and funeral directors can be recommended by the embassy. There are only a few well-maintained burial sites in Thailand and they are mostly reserved for the expat Chinese who are sometimes housed in permanently air-conditioned mini-tombs. If you, a mere foreigner, insist on your beloved being properly buried in a marked grave, you'll likely have to go to the expense of transportation by air back to your home country.

Cultural expectations at cremations can produce some nasty shocks. A family waited behind at a Pattaya temple to collect the ashes of a recently dead Brit. When the small urn was at length delivered to the distressed wife she couldn't resist opening it immediately only to let out a loud scream as she dropped the box and its contents on the floor. For there, on top of the ashes, lay her husband's false teeth which the thoughtful monastery staff had put to one side prior to the burning of the body. On another occasion, a still intact glass eye stared back at the family when the urn was opened back in the UK. Moreover, grinding machines are not usually in operation at Thai temples which can lead to sizeable pieces of bone being found in the urn. So shocking to the bereaved were these traumatic incidents that the Foreign Office began issuing warnings about different cultural norms concerning death in various countries.

Then there is the problem of wills which don't turn up. In the early 1990s a former British railways worker came to retire in Pattaya. His name was John Blyth and he brought with him an amazing collection of British train memorabilia including models of dozens of engines from the pre-nationalization era, rare timetables and even rarer photos. He began to write a weekly column in a local newspaper Pattaya Mail frankly of interest only to railway enthusiasts. Sadly his health declined seriously after a few years and he became extremely bad-tempered and aggressive leading to a total abandonment by his once-large circle of expat friends. Living alone and ill in a modest two-room apartment in Pattaya, he was an easy victim for his Thai acquaintances to empty his bank account and abuse his credit cards. He ended up very sick, destitute and totally miserable. His flat was very dirty and the apartment-block owner demanded that he quit the premises without further ado. To her the railway gems were just unwanted clutter.

When I first visited John at the request of the embassy, which had been contacted by the angry apartment-block owner wanting to get rid of an unwelcome tenant, a tragic sight met my eyes. He had no money, hadn't eaten for days and was lying in his own urine and faeces. The owner wanted him out of the flat and never to return on the excuse that his rent was substantially in arrears. I managed to get John admitted to the local public sector hospital in Naklua for a couple of days where it was discovered that he was suffering from terminal cancer. The embassy made attempts to discover the identity of his next of kin from the evidence provided in his previous passport applications, but the result was a total blank. It seemed that John was completely alone. Even in his lucid moments, the unfortunate guy did not want to talk to me about his past or his family.

The last thing the hospital wanted was a patient on their hands without any financial resources to pay the bill. By a stroke of good fortune I managed to find a home for mentally ill Thais in northern Thailand – not that John was mentally ill but beggars can't be choosers – which agreed to take him whilst we continued to try and track down any relatives or friends who might want to help. John was well aware what was happening to him and cursed me as the culprit who, he felt, had forcibly moved him from his Pattaya flat. However, he did once mention unexpectedly that he had a will which contained all manner of useful information. Unfortunately, he could not remember where it was but he was sure it was somewhere safe in Thailand in a locked drawer.

John did not survive long in the bleak northern Bangkok accommodation and died two weeks later. I made a determined attempt to track down the will by literally ransacking the smelly Pattaya flat in the company of two bemused Thai police officers, visiting several Thai lawyers who specialized in making wills, advertising in the local press and even appearing on two cable TV interviews. Surely somebody somewhere must know something. I even contacted several societies in UK catering for British train enthusiasts. But nothing of significance emerged. In the meantime the owner of the apartment had cleared it of all the railway treasures, dumped in the rain for the local refuse collection, and conducted a major fumigation in readiness for the next tenant. John was given a pauper's cremation which nobody attended. The Bangkok temple in question regularly burns penniless deceased souls, six at a time. Sightings of ghosts are particularly frequent in that area.

Two years later I received a phone call from a Pattaya lawyer who said he had the will of a certain John Blyth. He wanted to know if I knew of his whereabouts. The will, properly drawn up in Thai some years previously with an English translation, stated that under no circumstances was he to be cremated but transported back to England for burial in southern England. The document gave details of the railway memorabilia with an estimated auction value of more than forty thousand pounds with an instruction that it be donated to a named transport museum in the UK. All too late of course. John's case illustrates very well that if you do make a will in Thailand, then make sure some reliable person knows where to find it quickly once you have shuffled off this mortal coil.

Some deaths are the subject of litigation especially where the expired Brit has an estate in Thailand or in UK or both. The embassy does not involve itself in legal battles of this sort but does keep a list of suggested lawyers. A British guy died in Pattaya but the two sides of his family became locked in a bad-tempered argument about ownership of his luxurious villa in the resort which remains unresolved many years later. There was also a suspicion that the deceased had kept a large security box in a local Pattaya bank which was rumoured to be an Aladdin's cave of mega-cash, antiques and expensive jewels. Thai lawyers had a field-day raking in huge fees as they kept the warring factions at bay.

Eventually I was asked to be an impartial witness at the opening of the bank vault along with representatives of the families, several lawyers and three Thai police officers. Expectations rose and hearts began to beat when the bank manager produced not one but two steel boxes which were duly opened with double-keys in an extraordinarily long drawn-out ceremony involving photographers and an endless stream of documents to sign. But hopes were duly dashed when one box just contained an old copy of a British newspaper The Daily Sport and an extremely stale, half-eaten cheese sandwich, whilst the other produced merely a pornographic magazine with the lacklustre title Lolita in Bangkok.

Sometimes the dead do indeed have the last word.

SEVEN: PLAYING DOCTORS AND NURSES

Thailand has a lot to offer when it comes to medical treatment. The best of the private sector institutions measure up to the standards of care and of the latest technology which are found in Western Europe and the United States. Those Thai universities with a faculty of medicine have often attracted glowing reports internationally for their research projects. Over one million foreigners from all over the world visited Thailand last year as medical tourists, paying for the whole range of options from heart-bypass surgery and joint replacements to cosmetic surgery and wellness packages.

It's a fair assumption that most British tourists visiting Thailand don't expect to end up in hospital. Up to half of British visitors risk travelling to the Land of Smiles without any medical insurance whatsoever. Others do have limited travel insurance, bought along with the air ticket at the travel agent back in UK, but this may not be sufficient to cover any serious mishap resulting in hospitalization. There is still a UK-based medical insurance policy in common use today which specifically excludes from cover "any illness which is not holiday-related". This ambiguous restriction, as may be imagined, has been the cause of much personal and financial anxiety. One man was refused cover after he was bitten by a rabid dog. The argument of the underwriter was it could have happened anywhere, not necessarily on vacation.

Expats based in Thailand for most or all of the year tend to worry rather more than tourists about being covered for medical costs. Indeed, the most frequent speakers at Pattaya's weekly expat clubs are representatives of hospitals and local insurance agents selling their packages. Many of the British expats in Pattaya are male retirees in their 60s and 70s facing the problem that insurance companies love you less and less as you get older. Some companies boast that they never kick out ageing subscribers, but that of course assumes that the customers can continue to pay the ever-rising premiums. A comprehensive medical insurance for a British man of 70, even if he has had a reasonable health record to date, can now be in the region of four thousand pounds a year. Maybe more.

Ageing expats without adequate medical cover pose a problem of deep concern to Thai hospitals in the publicly-funded sector. Aliens are expected to pay for their own bills or to have access to people who can. Several public hospitals in Bangkok, Phuket and Pattaya have been complaining recently that they are millions of baht out of pocket with unpaid bills by foreign visitors and expats. There have even been suggestions of late that long-stay retirement visas in Thailand should only be awarded to foreigners with adequate medical cover. In practice, such a policy would be very difficult to enforce especially as the phrase "adequate medical cover" is a notoriously ambiguous term.

A few years ago there was the celebrated case of a British man who dropped dead of a heart seizure in the car park of the immigration bureau shortly after delivering his "all-clear" medical certificate from a local hospital in connection with his work permit application. I once saw a doctor's note for a man suffering from terminal cancer which stated that the only known illness was elephant's foot disease. Doubtless money had changed hands.

Shortly before my retirement from embassy work, I attended a conference at Chonburi General Hospital to which all foreign embassies had been invited to discuss their policies when one of their nationals fell ill. Only three embassies bothered to turn up – the Norwegian, the American and the British – and all stated that they do not pay medical bills under any circumstances. The hospital authorities countered that foreign embassies simply could not wash their hands of the problem as Thailand cannot afford to treat aliens without any hope of recompense. The conference, needless to say, was a total waste of time. Indeed I was delighted that I had taken along a projector and promotional video of the wonders of the Tower of London for the foreign tourist and the history of the House of Windsor which at any rate filled in forty minutes of a truly fruitless morning.

British government research suggests that Thailand is in the top three countries of the world where Brits are likely to find themselves in hospital. The main reasons are the high incidence of traffic accidents on Thailand's roads, particularly those involving motorbikes, and the existence of large numbers of elderly expats who are at risk from lifestyle diseases including cancer and hypertension-related conditions. The problem is that young men on holiday tend to ignore the possibility of physical injury whilst elderly expats are dealing with the reality that, sooner or later, insurance companies will reject them or raise the premiums to horrific levels. If we live long enough we all have to become our own insurer.

In 2007 I met Dave. He was a 25 year-old junior computer programmer from Luton in UK and came to Thailand with two mates for what was indeed to prove to be the holiday of a lifetime and one he's not likely to forget. Dave rented a motorbike and was involved in a serious road accident when he charged up a one-way Pattaya street the wrong way in the middle of the night. He was rushed unconscious by the Sawangboriboon public rescue service to the nearest private-sector hospital where staff explained to his worried mates that they needed proof of valid insurance or alternatively one hundred thousand baht (around two thousand pounds) just to begin tests and emergency treatment. The alternative was a transfer to a public hospital where doctors would try to make him comfortable and not much more. Regrettably Dave had no insurance apart from limited travel cover if he happened to be involved in an air disaster or lost his luggage.

All the Pattaya hospitals kept my mobile telephone number for emergencies of this sort and I arrived early in the morning to see what could be done. Dave's friends, who themselves were travelling on a tight budget, did produce the home telephone number of Dave's parents in UK which was immediately relayed by me to the 24-hours emergency consular service in London. Although it was still the middle of the night in England, the parents luckily answered the phone and agreed to transfer to the hospital by Western Union two thousand pounds to start the medical ball rolling.

On the medical front Dave was saved. His parents eventually paid over seventy thousand pounds just for two operations to repair his broken legs as well as treatment of other injuries. He was in hospital for over a month and was lucky not to have sustained brain injuries as he was not wearing a crash helmet at the time of impact. Incidentally, even if he had been insured, the company might have voided or reduced the claim because he had not taken full precautions by forgetting to wear head gear. As Dave regained full consciousness, it began to dawn on him that he might easily have been dead by now without the vital consular contact with his parents.

Then the thunderbolt struck. One morning I was summoned to the hospital bursar's office where two Thai policemen were sat holding a wad of papers. They explained that Dave had actually collided with a young Thai motorcyclist at the scene of the accident who remained in a critical condition at a public sector hospital as he didn't have the money for a more expensive facility. Moreover, the police said, Dave had driven the wrong way up a street whilst there was clear medical evidence in a blood test that he had been drinking heavily. Dave's passport had thus been confiscated by the police pending a legal outcome. If the case went to court, we were soberly warned, a term of imprisonment in a Thai jail was a distinct possibility.

When problems like this appear, the embassy's policy is to suggest that Brits in trouble contact a Thai lawyer. In view of the seriousness of the situation, Dave's father flew over on the next available flight. The lawyer explained that a criminal prosecution could well ensue for drunk and dangerous driving and that, because of the long delays inherent in the Thai system, Dave might have to remain in Thailand for many months for the court hearings even to start. Dave's father tried to argue that the police had no right to hold his son's passport but the point is trivial as Dave had already been placed on the banned exit list held on computers at Thai airports and border posts. Whether you have your passport or not is no longer the point when dealing with the Thai police. It's a question of whether your details have been flagged on the immigration records.

Eventually a civil settlement was reached whereby Dave's family paid for the medical bills of the injured Thai man and gave compensation for his notional loss of earnings. There were also substantial lawyer's fees and, of course, "tea money" for the police to drop the charges which is a normal procedure in controversial cases such as this. The final cost, including Dave's own hospitalization, was just over two hundred thousand pounds. I was told that the family needed to remortgage the family home in UK to raise the mega-cash. Although Dave' case was one of the most serious hospital cash crises I was called upon to monitor, it was by no means unique.

On a separate issue, Thai law in 2010 was changed to allow for the introduction of living wills. Thai doctors don't like to talk about the possibility of death and are reluctant to give a straight answer when the subject comes up. The tradition in Thailand has been to continue treatment until a person actually dies, although in practice this is more the custom in private hospitals than in public institutions where the patients tend to be poorer.

Once seriously-ill private patients are no longer able to pay the fees and have nobody else to provide funds, it's normal for the hospital authorities to arrange a transfer to a public sector hospital "to be made comfortable". In these circumstances, death is not uncommon.

The real advantage of a living will is when a person is unconscious, for example by a heart attack or following a traffic accident, and is thus unable to direct his or her own treatment for long periods of time. Basically a living will means that you don't want to be kept alive when all hope of recovery is gone.

Vacationers are very unlikely to bring a living will with them but expats in Thailand are beginning to keep a signed copy with their own papers or filed at their favourite hospital. I saw the living will come into play in just one case. A 76 year old Brit had a serious stroke, was without insurance or substantial assets, but had a son in UK who travelled out to see his father. A search of the flat by the son did indeed reveal a living will specifying that no life-support machine be used in case of chronic ill-health. Although the father's prospects were poor and the family did not have substantial resources anyway, the living will was a clean way to end the suffering process. The alternative was to move the terminally-sick pensioner to a public hospital, involving a journey by bumpy ambulance of maybe 30 miles, where he would have expired in any case.

One day I received a phone call from a senior policeman in Pattaya to say that he was grateful for the assistance I had recently given in a complex case involving a confidence-trickster posing as a qualified doctor and another concerning a tourist found murdered in a taxi on his way from the airport. The officer said that he wanted to express his thanks by inviting me to the Royal Thai Police Hospital in Bangkok where an important meeting would be held. I did not appreciate at the time that I was one of the few foreigners ever to be invited to witness – wait for it – a Thai autopsy! Apparently observing an autopsy is part of the training for some policemen although I don't think it is usual for diplomatic personnel. I was advised by a colleague in the embassy that it might not be a good idea to refuse this educational opportunity. "You can take it Barry," was the general drift of the argument.

The procedure was to stand in line with eight nervous-looking young policemen, all of us in white garb and surgical masks, whilst the forensic pathologist went about his work with a variety of tools which made a loud noise, especially the circular saw. Two of the observing policemen passed out during a particularly gruesome drilling procedure and another had to leave the room to be sick. I was congratulated at the end of the ordeal and even given a certificate of competence for having remained standing throughout the ordeal. What nobody knew was that I was very short-sighted at the time, prior to having corrective surgery a year or so later, which meant that when I removed my thick glasses, which I did very early in the autopsy, I couldn't discern anything that was happening on the cold slab some yards away.

Myopia has its attractions.

EIGHT: THE TRAGIC AND THE BIZARRE

The British Foreign Office expends a lot of effort telling its nationals going abroad what's possible and what isn't. Embassies can issue you with replacement travel documents and provide some help if you are the victim of a serious sexual or physical assault or find yourself seriously hospitalized. They can contact you if you are detained in a police station or prison overseas and offer to get in touch with friends or relatives anywhere in the world. They will willingly provide you with a list of local lawyers, interpreters, doctors or funeral directors but will warn you these suggestions are not "guaranteed by us". If you are involved in a forced marriage or are affected by parental child abduction, by all means contact your nearest consular section. But those latter issues are more likely to arise in India than in Thailand.

I dealt with only one rape case of a British national. A 25-year old Nottingham-born tourist Karen was backpacking her way round Asia and happened to end up in Pattaya. She was unlucky enough to hire a motorbike taxi for a short journey, but the driver decided to detour to a lonely wooded area where he raped her before taking her back to her hotel. An observant security guard there, noticing Karen's obvious distress and unkempt appearance with soil and leaves on her dress, took the number of the motorbike. No women police officers were available to be with Karen – it was six o'clock in the morning – so it was my perceived duty to take her to a local hospital for the medical examination, the taking of the swabs and the offer of a post-sex pill to reduce the chances of pregnancy.

In the meantime the young Thai man had been arrested. A senior policeman told him he was a disgrace to Pattaya and wasn't exactly helping in the marketing of the resort. The guy's black eye was testament to a somewhat rough interrogation. The wheels of justice can turn surprisingly quickly in Thailand, when the chips are really down and reputation of the whole country is at stake, and the court case was held within a week. Karen coped with the whole experience with calm and guts. The Thai man was sentenced to 10 years in prison, reduced to five because he pleaded guilty. In my whole embassy career I never saw a similar example of fast-track justice on this scale.

In overall terms there is much that embassies cannot do. They can't give legal advice or get involved in the outcome of court cases. They can't get you out of prison or request the police or the public prosecutor to drop criminal charges. They can't obtain better treatment for you in prisons or hospitals than that given to local people. And, of course, no cash handouts! So it's not surprising that the two most frequently-desired consular services were for me to get criminal cases quashed or to provide urgent financial help. Clearly not enough travellers are reading the Foreign Office's website advice Know Before You Go. That culture is all about pointing people in the right direction to help themselves. Spoon feeding is very much frowned on.

Of course there are exceptions to every rule. The British government, through the foreign secretary who has the prime overseas remit, is very concerned about the image of Britain abroad. If a client proves to be sufficiently high-profile then a special case may be made out, provided that the matter has been thoroughly thrashed out in London. Take for example the tragedy of Samantha Orobator, born in Nigeria but a British national, who was jailed in an extremely grisly prison in the Laotian capital, Vientiane, on a heroin smuggling charge which results in a mandatory death sentence there. She was arrested in August 2008 and given a life sentence by Laos judges. She claimed to have impregnated herself clandestinely with a fellow prisoner's semen specifically in order to avoid the death penalty. Pregnant women are not executed in Laos. Samantha, who always maintained her innocence of the criminal charges, was deported to the UK in August 2009 to serve her sentence in a British prison. Eventually British judges reduced her sentence to 18 months under a judicial review authorized by the 1984 Repatriation of Offenders Act.

It was well-known at the time that Quinton Quayle, the then British ambassador to Thailand, (Laos was also in his brief) was closely involved in the case whilst Samantha was detained, personally visited her and helped in the repatriation bureaucracy. Rightly so in my view. There was evidence that threats and coercion had been used pre-trial in Samantha's case and that the Laos judges did not allow a proper defence submission. The conditions in Phonthong prison in Vientiane were appalling and medical facilities virtually non-existent. Two Nigerian men had coerced Samantha into carrying the drugs through Wattay airport, Vientiane, taking her passport and threatening to kill her if she refused to carry the heroin to Australia. Samantha was also allegedly assaulted and raped by these men.

But who has ever heard of Michael Newman, a British citizen who was found dead in his prison cell also in Phonthong prison in 2008? He had been arrested by Laos police for drugs offences as far back as 2003, howbeit for carrying amphetamines rather than heroin. According to Save A Life, a foreign prisoner support service based in UK, there had been repeated and unsuccessful requests to the British embassy over four years to negotiate a prisoner transfer agreement that would allow him to be repatriated to correctional facilities in UK. Of course, the two cases are very different. Michael Newman, unlike Samantha Orobator, was a career criminal also involved in "boiler room" scams in Thailand, elaborate conspiracies to defraud investors and gullible members of the public into parting with their cash. Samantha was well supported by her family and the black community in UK who campaigned vigorously and daily on her behalf. Michael Newman had no such support base in Britain and just an isolated Thai wife without any influential contacts. The point is simply that high-profile criminal cases are sometimes, repeat sometimes, treated differently by the British authorities from the less sensational or less controversial ones. But you have to know how to shout.

Every year the foreign office handles more than a million consular inquiries across the globe and more than 50,000 British nationals get into serious trouble of one sort or another. But some of the approaches are positively bizarre and, down in Pattaya, I certainly received my fair share of them. It's a fact of life that many tourists confuse embassy duties and responsibilities with a one-stop-shop facility covering literally anything. Some problems are actually language-based. Because English is widely spoken in Thailand, at any rate in the tourist areas, Brits commonly but wrongly suppose that the use of our global language means that Thais also understand our cultural norms. That's where matters start to go wrong.

As an example, take food and drink which do not appear on any known list of formal consular responsibilities but are taken very seriously by British visitors. A Scotsman once phoned me to ask my help in complaining at a five star hotel in Pattaya that the waiter had failed to bring him a ploughman's lunch (basically cheese, chutney and bread) which is a decidedly British treat.

"Surely everybody knows what a ploughman's lunch is," he growled as he surveyed what the nervous waiter had actually brought, namely two boiled eggs in a sharp chilli sauce.

In a similar case, a tourist from Doncaster complained that in his hotel in Jomtien a "full" English breakfast had included frogs' legs instead of crispy bacon. Perhaps he should have ordered the smaller version. A chef from Exeter once contacted me specially to find out if I could provide him with the recipe used for the wedding cake at Prince William's marriage ceremony. He was surprised to hear I had not actually been invited.

I had been in office for only a few weeks when a British woman from Derby explained in great irritation that she couldn't find Oxo cubes anywhere on the shelves of any supermarket in town. She was very angry with the hotel Thai receptionist who had informed her that they were definitely on sale at a certain store. However, when the lady scanned the shelves, she could find only Bovril. "It's not the same thing at all," she bleated. Personally I thought the hotel receptionist deserved a medal for apparently understanding something about Oxo cubes, a very British obsession in the first place. The only suggestion

I could offer to her was to visit Malaysia on a side-trip as the supermarkets there in Penang and Kuala Lumpur do stock such items as they are manufactured locally. The Notts lady was not best pleased by this advice and suggested I go on a proper training programme to improve the forlorn service being provided by the British government in Pattaya.

There was a wine expert from Worthing who visited Pattaya with his Filipina wife (whom I knew) and clearly wanted to impress her. They invited me to dine with them one evening at an expensive restaurant and ordered a bottle of red wine which came in a refrigerated state which, particularly a few years back, was decidedly not acceptable unless specifically requested.

Another bottle was speedily brought by the unsure young waiter who explained that he had been absent with flu on the very day that fridges and defrosting had been covered in his induction programme, thus leading to this particular faux pas. The new bottle was at room temperature and, after taking a couple of sips, our Worthing host confided that he wasn't sure whether the wine was from a German or French vineyard.

Calling over the still confused waiter, he asked him, "Go and find out where this wine came from will you?" The boy was absent for about five minutes before arriving back with the great news. "I have found out sir," he announced, "It came from Friendship supermarket round the corner."

Sex always loomed large in the bizarre annals of my consular experience. One guy from Manchester told me this was his first visit to Pattaya and that he wanted me to find him, "a good Thai lass, not too expensive and good in bed." He explained that he had already visited one of the local expat clubs and raised the same matter at the Any Questions forum, only to be told to "get stuffed". Sadly I could offer no better advice. Unfortunately, he was later robbed of his wallet and wrist watch after wandering down the resort's beach road in the middle of the night and agreeing to a street walker's offer to provide horizontal leisure pursuits in his hotel room. There he discovered that the lady had an Adam's apple, not to mention an unwelcome appendage lower down, and ordered her to leave immediately. She did so but with his wallet hidden in her knickers. In Pattaya the written caution on some food products "Warning May Contain Nuts" takes on a new meaning.

An elderly tourist from Cardiff came to me one morning at our newly-opened Pattaya office – an accommodation saga in itself and described in a later chapter – and began mumbling with one hand over his mouth that I needed to "do something". After a few seconds I realized that he was not wearing his dentures which made communication difficult. I suggested he write down the bones of his story and he explained that he had taken a female go-go dancer back to his hotel room where congress of some kind had occurred. The Welshman then fell asleep and discovered next morning that his new companion had disappeared, taking with her the set of false teeth standing in a glass in the bathroom as well as a number of Steradent tablets and a tube of Polygrip Ultra. The Thai pickup had even left a scribbled note in rough English which indicated that her grandfather was still alive and badly needed the stolen items to improve his personal appearance in anticipation of an upcoming birthday.

The tooth fairy tale did not end there. I suggested I drive the distressed tourist visit a local dentist and request a new set of dentures as an emergency. However it was a public holiday and not many surgeries were open. The first dentist encountered said he was open only for extractions and could not cope with dentures on a Buddha day. The second one did agree to take the necessary impressions but said the new dentures would take a full week to make. This was no use as the Welshman had a return air ticket for three days hence.

In a final attempt to be helpful, I suggested the unfortunate guy return to the go-go bar that evening to ask for the return of the false teeth which were being sorely missed by their rightful owner. Alas this plan also collapsed when the club manager explained that the pole dancer in question had not reported for work as she had gone to northern Thailand for his grandfather's birthday. This saga illustrated to me that over-servicing clients with problems is not an advisable course of action in embassy work. Some weeks later I received a phone call from the Bangkok embassy saying that a complaint about me had been received from somebody in Wales and did I know anything about prostitution and teeth?

As the years rolled by, the list of bizarre incidents grew longer. They included a transvestite who told me that she had come to Thailand for breast enlargement but had run out of money halfway through the treatment. As a result one breast was much bigger than the other as well as much harder. Could I help out financially? I was also asked to translate a tattoo which had been indelibly put on a tourist's arm after he fell asleep and drunk in a tattoo parlour. In the same vein, I was approached to translate into plain English the ancient writing on the decaying walls of the Cambodian temples at Ankgor Wat which a tourist had captured with his zoom lens camera. I was even asked to assist in a visitor's hunt for Elvis Presley who was believed to be hiding out in Pattaya after a dummy successfully replaced him at his funeral in Memphis in 1977. Apparently Elvis was still very overweight after escaping from the coffin and was still addicted to hamburger joints. Thus the optimistic fan wanted me to check out Burger King on a daily basis whilst he kept an eye on McDonalds.

One of the oddest problems I encountered came on New Year's Day near the turn of the century. I received a phone call at 7 p.m. from a highly distressed British gentleman. He explained that he was completely stranded at a local zoo some miles out of town and without access to public transport. The story was that he had decided to take a closer look at the caged monkeys and had leaned a little too close. One of the monkeys, acting from boredom or annoyance, had snatched the glasses from his nose and dropped them into a pile of excrement at the bottom of the cage. It occurred to me, a wicked thought indeed, that this might be the supreme example of a Brit Literally in the Shit.

The distraught tourist continued that he had tried to rescue his spectacles by inserting his arm and hand through the bars, but the monkey in question was thwarting his attempts by snarling and threatening to bite with its decidedly unfriendly teeth. A bystander at the zoo then suggested he should go to the zoo office and report the untoward incident. After his banging on the door for five minutes, an elderly Thai security guard appeared and said everybody in authority had gone home as it was a public holiday. Sadly he had no keys to open the cages.

The problem now was that our friend was very short-sighted and could not drive back to Pattaya without his glasses. Luckily the crisis was resolved when the security guard offered to take him on the back of his motorbike for a princely sum which was at least ten times the going rate for motorbike transport. The next day was another public holiday so I hope the Gloucester guy had better luck with the opticians in town than the Cardiff one did with the dentists. I never did hear and I certainly never asked.

I had finally learned my lesson about not biting off more than you can chew.

NINE: THE RED LIGHT DISTRICT

Depending on which alleys and byways you choose to include on your tour, Pattaya's best-known entertainment district known as The Walking Street is about the same size as Vatican City. Views are divided about whether the similarity ends there or begins there.

With around three hundred bars, nightclubs, restaurants and convenience stores crowded into an area no bigger than a square mile, Walking Street's real-time history dates back to the late 1960s when the resort was a haven for holidaying US forces caught up in the war in Vietnam, Cambodia and Laos. The original 100 or so buildings were constructed illegally at the water's edge, some actually on stilts, and that remains their doubtful status to this day. Every seven years or so there is a court order to tear down these illegal structures, but TIT (This Is Thailand) so the demolition teams never actually show up.

The changes over the years have been enormous. No longer is English the solely dominant language spoken by visitors to the

Walking Street. You are just as likely these days to hear Russian, Japanese, Chinese and Hindi in what has become a veritable Tower of Babel. It's cosmopolitan and trendy which is why McDonald's opened a burger branch there in 2011.

New technology has also transformed the Walking Street. The neon-lit signs and colorful magic message boards become more sophisticated every year. There are umpteen videos on You Tube and endless discussions on Facebook. Trip Advisor has well over one thousand comments from the visiting public. These days everybody can be a journalist. Of a sort anyway.

The Trip Advisor remarks reveal there are three basic standpoints on Walking Street. The first is generally positive and finds the district appealing. Here's a recent contributor: "White cops, ladyboys, snake handlers, laughter, clowns, sexy ladies, mad punters, cold beer, warm beer, go-go, raunchy shows, kebab carts, bug carts. Loved it."

The negative responses include the headings "Detritus of humanity" and "Sodom and Gomorrah". You can guess the rest. There's also a feeling that this is not a nice place to take the kids or to enjoy a restful honeymoon. "I couldn't wait to get out of there," writes one disgusted traveller from the legendary Tunbridge Wells.

In the middle, of course, are the neutral respondents. Said one well-travelled guy, "I couldn't see what all the fuss is about. As long as you are reasonably broad-minded, Walking Street is fine. But it's not unique in the world. You don't have to touch, so just walk through and gawp at the street shows and the pouting tarts and transvestites."

Love it or hate it, Walking Street is still evolving. Ten years ago you might have been surprised to see a Turkish kebab stall or a disco specially tailored for Iranians.

But not any more. Nightly, large tour groups from mainland China and the island of Taiwan pass through, always under the direction of a leader carrying a colourful flag to reduce the chances of a tour member getting lost. These are the new Pattaya Daleks, always in groups, of limited vocabulary, eager to take orders and reluctant to spend any money. The Chinese embassy in Bangkok in 2010 started to advertise its emergency number on a huge video screen erected at the entrance to Walking Street. That's a sign of the times. The Chinese are coming.

Yes, Walking Street is the resort's best-known red-light district, but it's much more than that. It's a brightly-lit neon tourist attraction like so many others in the city. People stroll there to take in the sights, the smells and the sensations. Of the two thousand or so visitors on any one night, most are not looking for either sleaze or a horizontal encounter in a short-time hotel room. Many tourists bring the whole family, the same people who a few hours before were probably visiting the tropical gardens, the underwater zoo and the elephant show. The seafood restaurants and the live-music venues are full of foreigners enjoying an evening out before dutifully returning to their hotels. If you prefer your own company nobody will mind.

No single feature about Pattaya's Walking Street has generated more discussion than the presence of a large number of ladyboys at the south end of the main walkthrough area. The term ladyboy, khatoey in Thai, covers a wide range of men or former men. It can just mean an effeminate male – period. More usually the expression means a guy who has had some surgery, initially a nose-job or rhinoplasty, but it also covers breast implants, hormones, silicon injections, Adam's Apple reduction or even genital reassignment.

Civil rights for Thai khatoeys are few and far between. The luckier or cleverer ones have high visibility as actors on television shows and dramas, as fashion designers, hairdressers, dressmakers and make-up artists. Increasingly they are found as staff in restaurants or banks and, less visibly to the foreign tourist, in factories and industrial plants. But they all face potential job discrimination especially when their ID card photos don't match the look of their gender preference. In turn, many khatoeys have trouble obtaining a passport or a driving licence. Some can't even open a bank account.

So it's hardly surprising that some jobless ladyboys turn to petty crime to make ends meet, although most are not as violent as the Meat and Two Veg characters we met in an earlier chapter. They will openly approach males of any age and offer sex but they also know the chances of rejection are high: the majority of gay or straight men don't normally choose a transvestite as a partner. This is why the ladyboys quickly learn to remove the wallets or jewelry of males whom they try to lock in a fake embrace as their painted and experienced fingers dart into pockets likely to hold something of value. Others operate in groups of two or three as a motorbike gang. While one ladyboy engages a male in conversation and tries to embrace him, a second attempts to steal something of value whilst a third is parked nearby on a motorbike ready for the escape.

There are even instances where female prostitutes and ladyboys get together to plan a joint scam. Two young women accosted a British tourist on Walking Street and he foolishly agreed to accompany them for a threesome at an apartment in a remote district of Pattaya. Whilst indulging in horizontal carnal enterprises whilst watching a video Holly Does Houston, he did not realize that a ladyboy was hiding under the bed and searching his trousers which lay on the floor nearby. He only discovered what was missing after being given a "free" ride back into town by one of the young ladies on her motorbike. The scam was eventually uncovered by the police but not before a small fortune had been accumulated by means of this ingenious enterprise.

Policing on the Walking Street is primarily the responsibility of the Thai tourist police division. They operate nightly from a mobile unit at one end of Walking Street. Because only one or two regular officers are on duty on any given evening, both Thai and foreign police volunteers have been recruited for many years. Their general duties are to answer general tourist questions, sort out any minor problems and visit clubs or restaurants where there is a problem. If authorized by the regular Thai police officer on duty, the volunteers can apprehend people and escort them back to the mobile unit or the nearby sub-office for interrogation.

My role with the Pattaya tourist police began in the late 1990s when several embassy-related cases required liaison. One involved the death of a serial pedophile and another was an amazingly complicated and rare child abduction controversy. I suggested at that time that some foreigners based in Pattaya might have useful skills to assist the tourist police, such as linguistic ability to act as translators or relevant experience in undercover work or in drugs-busting. Although the notion of unpaid, foreign auxiliary police was certainly a controversial one, the idea took root and is today an accepted part of the law enforcement scene in Pattaya, Chiang Mai and Phuket.

In 2003 the group, which became known as Foreign Tourist Police Assistants (FTPA), began helping the regular officers in the Walking Street, based at a mobile unit or van at the major Beach Road entrance. Its main role was, and remains, to answer general tourist enquiries and to act as translators as and when necessary.

But FTPA officers, under the control of the Thai police officer in charge, do patrol the public areas of Walking Street and attempt to sort out any public order problems, usually related to drunkenness or disputes about the bill in a bar or club. The FTPA was the subject of a famous TV documentary series in 2008 named Big Trouble in Thailand, extracts of which are still available on You Tube.

In recent years the FTPA has attempted to become more professional by introducing strict rules about membership and behaviour. New recruits now have to be in possession of a one-year visa, provide evidence of a non-criminal background in their first country (as well as Thailand) and undergo a substantive observation and training programme. As the Walking Street has changed, so has the composition of FTPA which in late 2013 numbered around fifty auxiliary officers. There are now more Russian, Farsi and Arabic speakers, for example, who can speak to tourists in their own language and offer advice.

FTPA duties are also becoming more diverse. There are motorbike and foot patrols in the more popular parts of the city and a new office is scheduled to open on Beach Road to be shared with the marine police following a spate of unfortunate sea accidents in Pattaya bay. There is also a recently introduced "buddy" system in which pairs of Thai and foreign volunteers work together to improve effectiveness and to minimize any language misunderstandings with the general public. It should also be noticed that FTPA is not the only foreign group attached to the Thai police. There is also the FPV (Foreign Police Volunteers), a wholly separate organization, which is attached to the city police (not the tourist police) at Pattaya, Banglamung and Nongprue police stations. The FPV is currently run by Pattaya media mogul Niels Colov from Denmark.

What sort of people – usually men but women are very welcome – become FTPA auxiliaries? Most have a police or security background in their own country, but others bring complementary skills such as language proficiency or a diplomatic background. Of course, it's true that membership can attract undesirable elements. As T.S. Eliot wrote, "The last temptation is the greatest treason, to do the right deed for the wrong reason." But the disciplinary codes take care of the unwanted elements. Attempting to take bribes, wearing the uniform when not on duty, acting unprofessionally and using unauthorized violence are just some of the disciplinary offences leading to a formal inquiry and dismissal if the allegations are found to be true.

Of all the cases Ron's was the oddest and most exhausting. In the early days I was once called to the tourist police headquarters, then based on Pattaya's Second Road and not on the Buddha Hill where it is today, after an obvious tramp fell asleep on the concrete road in Walking Street and was removed at dawn by a considerate baht bus driver to a place of imagined assistance. On arrival I found an unwashed, balding person, aged about fifty, wearing a dirty T- shirt with the logo "Another Shitty Day in Paradise" and short pants which clearly had not seen soap and water for a long time. In these circumstances, the main task is to get the guy out of the tourist police station. The officers on duty are never interested in farang down-and-outs. I managed to lure the guy to a neighbouring cafeteria with the promise of bacon and eggs which the waitress said must be consumed at an outside table as the tramp might put the other customers off their meal.

Food, I have found, is a great liberator of the human tongue. Ron's northern accent revealed him to be British. He explained that he had come on holiday to Pattaya several weeks ago but had been cheated by a woman he met on Beach Road who had taken all his money and his passport. However, he did know the exact spot where she continued to sit every afternoon, presumably waiting for someone else to defraud. A quick check of his details at the immigration bureau revealed that Ron had in fact been in Thailand for two months, without a prior visa, and now had a serious overstay problem and no means of paying the fine.

The embassy in Bangkok was able to confirm that Ron had a sister in Blackburn. But she had washed her hands of him years ago and was not remotely interested in assisting her brother either spiritually or financially. Ron was unable to produce the names or details of anyone in the whole world who might want to help him.

In those days, the Foreign Office rules on spending cash on clients were not quite so strict and I managed to dump him with formal approval from my superiors in what I can only describe as a Thai doss-house overnight for the sum of one pound equivalent. I also bought him at the market a pair of shorts and a T-shirt.

The next afternoon Ron was looking slightly better and we set off to find the Thai lady on the Beach Road. Indeed she was there in her appointed spot, a young woman of about 25 wearing a polka dress, some cheap jewelry and a huge wooden cross hung round her neck which was reminiscent of the one Peter Cushing used to convert vampire Christopher Lee into dust in the old Dracula movie. She readily admitted that she had taken his passport in lieu of payment for sex some weeks before but denied she had stolen any money. I gave the stock embassy speel that it was an offence to withhold a British passport issued in the name of the Queen of England. Much to my surprise, this caused her to think.

At length she admitted that that the passport was hidden in her underwear but that she would retrieve the crucial documentation for as little as 1,000 baht or about twenty pounds. This offer was flatly contradictory to the embassy policy of never paying for anything controversial, let alone knicker contents, but I decided to risk my own cash and ended up paying her 10 pounds. At least Ron was reunited with his passport, but the problem of overstay and how to pay for the return flight remained.

The only solution for Ron was to give himself up to the city police for overstay, spend a couple of weeks in the local Pattaya jail and then transfer to the huge immigration jail in Bangkok. Here the embassy would assume some responsibility and, using a charity set up for the purpose, would repatriate him back to UK. But not quickly. The waiting time was months rather than days to convince naughty Brits not to repeat the offence. Ron's passport would likely be confiscated in UK and not returned until he had paid off what he owed to the British government.

I managed to persuade Ron that his best course of action was to surrender for overstay, explaining that at least he would eat in confinement pending an eventual flight home. And so it turned out. Four months later Ron was on a flight to UK after what I assumed would be just about the worst experience of his life.

Therefore, imagine my surprise soon afterwards when I received from the embassy an unopened letter with a postmark Blackburn marked for my attention. It was indeed from Ron who apologized but explained he was a Manchester University lecturer doing research on what happens to British tramps abroad. I had been set up well and truly and the sister was part of the conspiracy. Included with the letter was a ten pound note.

Presumably this was for my unauthorized expenditure for the contents of the knickers.

TEN: SPRINGTIME FOR HITLER

It's hard to imagine Hitler and the Third Reich having anything in common with the international playground known as Pattaya. In the 1930s the nazi regime closed down all the seedy nightclubs which had been truly infamous in the heady days of the Weimar Republic in the previous decade. It is true that senior SS chief Reinhard Heydrich ordered one Berlin establishment – Salon Kitty's – to remain open but this was to enable the Gestapo to monitor the visitors, especially diplomats, and to record with hidden microphones what they were saying in the bedrooms. Blackmail with espionage included was the name of the game at Salon Kitty.

None the less Hitler, with his silly moustache and stiff-armed salute, was still making waves in Thailand as late as mid-2013. Tales of a Bangkok fast food restaurant using a picture and a model of the late Fuhrer in its marketing campaign were still being debated on the internet. Hot on the heels of Hitler's fried chicken – of course he was a vegetarian in real life – came the students of Chulalongkorn University who erected a massive graduation banner in the middle of their campus that featured an image of the him giving nazi salute along with Batman, Superman and several other cartoon characters. A tipster who described himself as a concerned and incredulous American student asked the obvious question why the elite at a prestigious Thai institution would want to share their graduation celebrations with a mass murderer. The answer, I think, is a complex one for Europeans to understand.

One morning in October 2009 I was woken up at five in the morning by an anxious phone call from a Thai friend who worked at the soon-to-be-opened Louis Tussaud's wax museum in one of Pattaya's prominent malls the Royal Garden Plaza.

"You come at once to Sukhumvit Road and meet Adolf Hitler," was the alluring instruction and he rang off before I had any chance to question him further.

I did glance at my wrist watch to check it wasn't April Fool's Day. Sukhumvit, by the way, is the long and broad coastal highway which runs the whole way along Thailand's eastern seaboard from Bangkok to Trat for about 400 kilometers.

It turned out that the museum had hired a marketing company which had suggested that huge billboards should be erected along Sukhumvit near Pattaya to advertise the latest tourist attraction offered by the fast-developing city. As I drove along the highway I noticed two huge hoardings promoting recently-deceased singer Michael Jackson and martial arts expert Bruce Lee both looking down sternly on the passing traffic. But the third promotion was a huge picture of Adolf Hitler giving the fascist salute and emblazoned with the alarming expression in Thai "Hitler Is Not Yet Dead!" There had been several near-accidents as foreign drivers gawped in astonishment.

Assembled at a nearby cafe were several officials from Louis Tussaud's and the marketing company, all with worried looks on their faces. They explained to me that they had received complaints from both the German and the Israeli embassies in Bangkok that promoting Hitler in this way was totally unacceptable and demanding that the offending billboard be removed immediately.

Apparently I had been summoned to the cafeteria as I knew something about embassies in general and might be able to advise them what to do next in what could only be described as a unique crisis. I was also asked if the British embassy was likely to send them a complaint but I thought this was unlikely as Hitler wasn't a British passport holder and never had been.

What became clear almost at once was that the Thai marketing gurus had no idea who Hitler was, what he stood for and the fact that he had a major role in the annihilation of at least 50 million people during the early 1940s. I explained a little bit about Auschwitz and the sensitivity of the issue known as the Holocaust, especially in Germany and Israel. One of the marketing company's representatives said that he was aware Hitler was a controversial figure but that was all the more reason for using him in publicity campaigns to attract attention. I replied that's OK as long as you are prepared for a succession of hostile publicity which could well affect income at the museum and shorten the queues at the ticket booth. Also, revenue-orientated City Hall officials would not be pleased to be embroiled in an acrimonious debate about European arch-villains of the past during the tourist high season.

The controversy in reality was short-lived. The organizers apologized to the embassies concerned and held a press conferences to explain that no offence had been meant and that, in the actual museum, Hitler's effigy appeared in the chamber of horrors with other mass murderers and not in the hall of fame along with Queen Elizabeth and President Bush. Meanwhile Hitler's billboard was quickly covered with sheets by local authority workmen and then dismantled at dead of night. The actual wax image of the Fuhrer in Louis Tussaud's museum suffered some rough handling by the early paying visitors on the first day of opening. Somebody managed to saw off Hitler's hands with a penknife and his iron cross (first class) was stolen to be replaced by the well-known expletive obscenity pinned on the vacant spot on his jacket. I'm told that in more recent times his effigy has disappeared altogether to make way for more recent villains such as the assassinated Osama bin Laden and the newish North Korean leader Kim Jong-un, but I can't vouch for these policy decisions.

The real point is that the use of nazi icons, memorabilia and celebrities does not have the same emotional appeal in Asia as it does in Europe. Hitler never visited Thailand, or even mentioned it so far as we know, although Heinrich Himmler is said to have sent scientists here to investigate whether or not there were any signs of the biological origins of pure Aryan mankind, the kind that the nazi movement wanted to encourage. However, the expedition failed to find any blue-eyed blond youths and lasses in Bangkok and returned to Berlin with their tales between their fascist legs.

One the other hand, one could never imagine Tussaud's in Thailand erecting a promotional billboard for Hideki Tojo, the Japanese general hanged in Tokyo for war crimes in 1948. That's much closer to home and there was a collaborationist pro-Japan government in Bangkok during the Second World War.

Although Thailand did not suffer anything like the horrors of the Japanese occupation of, say, the Philippines or Singapore, most well-educated Thais have at least some awareness of their own past. As for knowledge of European history, that's a very different matter.

The nazi theme actually goes back further than you might think in Thailand's entertainment industry. In the 1980s Bangkok newspaper columnist Bernard Trink wrote of a bar where your gin and tonic was served by young Thai women in jackboots and black uniforms. He advised everyone to "mosey on over" even if just for a single visit. There was also a Bangkok bar Germany Calling run by an Englishman with a sentimental attachment to the treasonable William Joyce, the American-born pro-nazi broadcaster, who was the last US citizen ever hanged by the British and one of the few prisoners awaiting execution who actually gained weight in the condemned cell. The bar served cocktails with fascist-sounding names such as Tokyo Rose sling, Hitler Punch and Bloody Eva Braun on the menu. But it soon closed down after freelance journalists in Bangkok reported the sensitive matter to the tabloid press in London. Incidentally the Englishman who ran Germany Calling later returned to Thailand and opened a diving training school in Pattaya. He was deported in 2007 for working without an authorized permit and for visa overstay. Whilst detained at Pattaya police station, he asked me whether there was any chance he could be appointed as my embassy deputy as he felt he understood human beings.

"You can always fill in a form," I suggested helpfully.

Even potato crisps have managed to get into the act. In the late 1990s there was an advertising campaign in Bangkok and

Pattaya for a certain brand which appeared to show a smiling Hitler accepting a crisp from no less a figure than Charlie Chaplin. Given that Chaplin in real life had lampooned and mimicked the Fuhrer in a film The Great Dictator, for which he had been placed on the Gestapo death list, and was widely suspected of having communist sympathies, this particular dalliance was most unlikely to say the least. Following a fuss from the German and Israeli embassies once again and a number of indignant letters in the local press, the advertisement was withdrawn from hoardings and public transport vehicles. But the issue set a remarkable precedent for the 2009 Hitler billboard controversy.

For several years there was a stall in the Pattaya's Made in Thailand Market, on Second Road, which sold nazi memorabilia, mainly fake iron crosses, imitation armbands and the like. A British guy Alan Grayson operating the stall also offered for sale pro-nazi books, for example Arthur Butz' Hoax of the 20th Century which is a wandering diatribe proclaiming holocaust denial and arguing the gas chambers in occupied Poland were a myth. There were also several books by right-wing historian David Irving downplaying Hitler's personal responsibility for atrocities or highlighting allied misdeeds such as the carpet bombing of Dresden in 1945. Not surprisingly you may think, Alan was one of Pattaya's early condominium jumpers and leapt to his untimely death in 2005 after going bankrupt. His disorganized flat was full of nazi-related stuff and the Thai police, perhaps not understanding the significance of the Third Reich, donated the lot in several suitcases to the Pattaya old people's home. I have often wondered what the pensioners there did with the photos of Himmler and the SS runes.

There still exists in Naklua a shophouse unit fronted by a Thai craftsman who paints exclusively portraits of the leaders of the Third Reich. Hitler is the most popular choice followed by Himmler and Goring. The entire business is export-orientated, mainly to mainland Europe, Germany and Hungary in particular. I went to see the painter Khun Toon in connection with the suicide of Alan Grayson and he told me that business is booming especially in those European countries where populism is on the rise as economic problems mount. I also found out that the oil paintings, which are very good quality, are doctored with special substances to age them artificially. So a Hitler made in Thailand 2013 is actually being marketed and sold in Europe as a Hitler made in Germany 1939. The Third Reich still provides a good living for a select few in contemporary Pattaya.

Yes, the Hitler phenomenon in Pattaya still lives. You still see on the roads motorbike drivers, both Thais and foreigners, sporting nazi style helmets and swastika patches or T-shirts. The Thais may not appreciate the significance of their adornments, but the farangs certainly do. A male go-go dancer in Pattaya's Boyztown during his meal break regularly wears a vest with a huge black swastika emblazoned on it. He has no idea what it means but says it was given to him by a German customer. He doesn't wear it during the dancing sessions round a chrome pole as vests are discarded during the professional entertainment. Still, so far as is known, no foreign embassies have chosen to become involved in the sale of militaria-related items or the preferences of lightly-clad entertainers. Only Hitler's public picture, it seems, moves foreign embassies to action.

Pattaya is a place where you can have Welcome American Navy tattooed on your thighs ready for the next full-moon party.

Nobody would bat an eyelid here if you started a remembrance society for Ghengis Khan or opened up the first oriental branch of the Flat Earth Society. There is one guy in Pattaya who rides his bike daily with a tame parrot perched on his shoulder, oblivious to the exhaust fumes and general pandemonium on the resort's roads. Pattaya is perhaps the only place in the world where an advertiser in a newspaper wrote he was looking for a home for his performing cat – it could jump through hoops on request – as he was about to undergo a two-year jail sentence and had failed in his attempt to get the adored feline included in the jail term. There is even a photo booth which specializes in making you look 30 years younger with makeup, wigs and cosmetics designed to impress your contacts on Facebook or whatever. Cash is king in Pattaya.

There's even a joke-video on You Tube, using voice-over material from the 2004 movie Downfall starring Bruno Ganz, about Hitler buying a condominium unit in Pattaya and then discovering to his horror that it has no sea view and is in a bad location.

So the Louis Tussaud marketing guru was right all along. Hitler Is Not Dead Yet.

ELEVEN: BE UPSTANDING IN COURT

It's a regular refrain in this book that Thai institutions and norms can be very different from their British counterparts. This is one of the reasons why Brits sometimes misjudge a situation. They are looking for a repeat of what would happen in their own country. When this does not happen, the results can be traumatic indeed.

Let's take the example of Frank, a first-timer in Thailand. He was 26 and came with a group of Brits to enjoy the pleasures of Pattaya. One evening, shortly after midnight, he was enjoying himself drinking beers and dancing in a crowded night club on the Walking Street when he was approached by one of the establishment's security guards. He told Frank that a Thai female customer in the club had complained that he had touched her breasts and patted her bottom in a totally uninvited way. The Brit denied the allegation. The young woman remained adamant. The tourist police were called.

Back at the tourist police mobile unit on Walking Street, the Thai woman said that Frank had bought her a drink, then invited her to dance and subsequently committed the indecent offence on the crowded dance floor. She said she was neither a staff member nor a prostitute and insisted that she had lost face with her friends and felt humiliated. The lady added that she was not interested in financial compensation but wanted a criminal prosecution.

Frank replied that he had a vague recollection of buying the woman a drink but had certainly not invited her to dance. In any case the dance floor was very crowded that night and it was well nigh impossible to tell who was associating with whom. The CCTV footage taken by the in-house cameras was inconclusive as sadly is often the case in circumstances such as these. CCTV installation is required in every club by law, but the new technology often seems to be strangely out-of-order when needed. A loud argument ensued between the Thai woman and Frank with expletives in Thai and English being bandied about frequently on both sides.

I happened to be on duty that night as an FTPA (Foreign Tourist Police Assistant) and the Thai police officer in charge of the mobile unit asked me to brief Frank on his situation. I explained that this was a case of a tourist's word against a Thai and that it was crucial, if at all possible, for an agreement to be reached on the spot. If not, Frank would be taken to the city police headquarters where arrest and incarceration were a distinct possibility. It might be better, I said, if Frank apologized as he could not be sure he had not accidentally touched the woman on the crowded dance floor.

But Frank refused point-blank. "I would sooner go to jail than admit I touched that woman," he stated.

The Thai police officer in charge then suggested he pay a small monetary award, about 20 pounds or 1,000 baht, to the woman as a way of ending the proceedings. But Frank was in no mood for compromise and dismissed the possibility of an apology or a financial contribution or both.

I appealed to him for the last time, "Frank, you are on holiday and need to go back to England to resume your life. If you are prosecuted you will need bail or spend months in prison waiting for your case to come up in court. Your name in the meantime will be put on the banned exit list at airports and borders."

Inevitably, Frank was taken in handcuffs to the city police headquarters and the aggrieved Thai woman and three of her friends also arrived at the same time. The desk officer at the police station obviously knew the woman and they chatted and smirked happily before Frank was asked whether he wished to plead guilty or not guilty to the crime of indecent behaviour in a public place. He swore he was innocent but unfortunately he had no witnesses as his holiday companions were visiting another club at the time. The friends of the Thai lady confirmed in writing that she had indeed been groped in a disgusting manner. It was three against one.

The desk officer then passed the case to the criminal-inquiry police lieutenant on duty. He explained to Frank in broken English that the odds were stacked against him but that, if he pleaded guilty now, he would be free to leave the police station a free man provided he paid a fine of 30,000 baht, around five hundred pounds, in lieu of being convicted in the Thai court. The original 20 pounds pay-off had indeed swelled considerably now that the charge had become official. But Frank was adamant. He was innocent and would tell the judge so in due course.

Frank was taken to the police station lock-up upstairs. It was late on a Saturday night and the place was as overcrowded as the night club. But it was populated with very different clients, mostly drunks, drug addicts and alleged transvestite thieves. Although facilities have since improved a lot, the situation a few years ago in the lock-up was dire: no aircon, no proper toilet or privacy, lots of biting insects and nowhere to sleep except on the stone floor assuming you could find a place to lie down. The only other foreigner present was an elderly Frenchman, accused of buying a marijuana cigarette from a police agent, who perpetually sang the French national anthem until warned by the Thai inmates to shut up or face extremely unpleasant consequences. These could likely include a savage beating.

The following morning I went to see Frank in his new surroundings, taking the customary cold water bottles and ham and cheese sandwiches brought from my home. The free scraps provided in Thai centres of incarceration, typically a handful of rice with a fish skeleton or a fried chicken foot, will never qualify for the Good Food Guide by any stretch of the imagination. By now the effects of alcohol had completely worn off and Frank was seeing his predicament in the cold light of dawn. I explained that it might be too late now to settle the matter out of court and that he should consider giving the embassy permission to inform his parents of his predicament. However, he refused and said he would face the court the following morning. He had no money to pay for a Thai lawyer, his friends had not showed up (and never did help in any way whatsoever) and the Thai bail-broker at the police station lost interest after Frank said he was without funds or collateral.

Under the law the Thai police have 48 hours before releasing a suspect, Thai or farang, or alternatively presenting him to the court. On the Monday morning Frank was taken with others by Black Maria in a chain-gang line to the Thai court and placed in the cells to await the judicial call. The judge heard the police reports and said, as expected, that he would remand Frank in custody or award bail in the sum of 100,000 baht or about two thousand pounds. The worst nightmare was coming true. Frank tried to explain to the judge (who understood English) that he was innocent, but the reply was that he must reserve his defence until the trial was eventually held.

Frank was remanded to Pattaya prison, a few kilometers out of town, where he spent the next three months awaiting the public prosecutor to digest the case and decide what further action to take. Every 12 days Frank was taken to Pattaya court for remand in accordance with Thai legal procedure. I visited him every few weeks – the embassy regulations said once every three months but this rule was not often followed in my time – and he did at length agree his parents in UK could be contacted. They said they were not wealthy but did send one thousand pounds to the embassy to cover extra food and prison comforts such as soap and to provide limited Thai legal representation at his trial.

When the trial date actually arrived, just short of four months after the alleged groping, Frank's case was quickly disposed of by the judge. Having heard the prosecution submission, based on statements made at the police station, and the statement of the defence lawyer who basically said the whole thing was a misunderstanding, Frank finally pleaded guilty. This was not because he felt blameworthy but was specifically in order to receive a lesser sentence which is the custom in Thai courts in those circumstances. He was fined 5,000 baht, about a hundred pounds, and ordered to be deported. Whilst awaiting deportation in a Bangkok immigration jail, the embassy arranged for a new air ticket funded by extra cash provided by his now panic-stricken parents.

Unluckily, the penalty for Frank did not end with his arrival back in the UK. His employers, a haulage company, had obviously found out about the Thailand debacle when he had not shown up for work after his supposed holiday. He was dismissed from his job, sought compensation in the British industrial court but lost partly on the ground that he had pleaded guilty to a crime whilst abroad! The point worth emphasis is that the whole matter could have been settled at the tourist police mobile unit in Pattaya for 20 pounds. The total financial costs to Frank's family at the end of the day exceeded four thousand pounds. Not to mention the damage to Frank's career history and the trauma to himself and his family. Indeed, his father suffered a fatal heart attack the following year which may well have been connected to these tragic events.

Frank's case underlines the truism that Thailand's criminal justice system is far different from Britain's. In Thailand, there are no juries and there are long waits in the clogged-up judicial system. Bail is available equally to Thais and foreigners but tends to be more expensive for the latter in some cases "lest they run away". Once a trial is held, weeks or months may expire before the next hearing. Unlike in Britain, the Thai court does not hear evidence one day after the other until the case is concluded. Indeed, if Frank had not finally pleaded guilty at his trial, the judge would have set the next hearing for 10 weeks later leading to a further period of pre-trial incarceration. A drugs case I know lasted from

2000 to 2008 waiting for the decisions of the provincial court, the appeal court and the supreme court.

In the Thai criminal courts documentary evidence is very important and verbal evidence less so than in British proceedings. To have stood any chance, Frank would have needed written statements from witnesses giving his side of the story. In the circumstances described, that was impossible. Of course, all documents must be in Thai or translated officially into the language. Attorneys for the prosecution and for the defence are extremely deferential to the judge who, in the absence of juries, is an all-commanding figure. During the course of my embassy career, I attended many court hearings and never once did I hear a serious quarrel between opposing lawyers during formal cross-examination. No similarity whatever with the British TV series Judge John Deed! A final difference between the Thai and British systems is that there is no verbatim report of the proceedings in Thailand. The judge speaks into a tape recorder or whatever to give a summary of what has been said.

Sometimes the outcome of a legal battle was better than expected for the defendant. Paul was a 58-year old Londoner who had taken early retirement as a teacher in England and decided to settle in Thailand where he intended to marry his Thai girlfriend of many years standing. He even followed a Thai ministry-recognised teachers' course to enable him to teach in Thai schools and colleges. In due course he became a father and his life seemed good, very good. He was one of those foreigners who could drive daily down Pattaya's sunny Beach Road on his way to work and feel great. He was internally gratified that he had left England for good.

But one evening Paul was returning home in the family car with the wife. They had been out for dinner with friends at the highly prestigious grill room of the Royal Cliff Beach Resort when a motorbike suddenly emerged at top speed from a side road and struck the driver's side of Paul's car. The motorcyclist was a Thai man in his 20s. He was dead. A crowd soon formed round the scene of the accident and Paul was taken to a hospital for what turned out to be minor cuts and bruises and considerable trauma. His wife was unhurt.

Paul's insurance company took care of most of the paperwork and obtained bail for him, but in due course the Thai mother and father turned up to ask what compensation Paul was going to pay them for killing their son.

The problem here is that most insurance policies set a very low limit of compensation in the case of death on the roads, less than two thousand pounds.

But the catch is that the tearful relatives do not have to accept such a paltry amount and can sue the driver separately in a civil action for a bigger cash sum. It was at this point that Paul contacted the embassy to ascertain what he should do. It seemed to me clear that no monetary compensation should be offered at this stage as it could be taken as a sign of guilt in any subsequent court hearings. The right way forward was to hire a good Thai lawyer. Luckily Paul was not too short of money.

It took some weeks for the Pattaya police to serve an indictment on Paul accusing him of reckless driving and causing the death of a third party. At the trial some months later the prosecution tried to argue that Paul was speeding, had been drinking and that his side lights and headlamps were not turned on. It was suggested that the young Thai's death was brought about by the car driver's culpability. There was even a hostile witness who claimed that Paul had gone through a red traffic signal about 30 seconds before the fatal clash.

In the event, the judge found Paul not guilty. The main reason was that his Thai wife had taken some very wise decisions early on. She had had the presence of mind immediately after the accident to take signed statements from three Thai witnesses who happened to be nearby and agreed that Paul was not driving too fast, that his dimmed headlights were on and that there was nothing he could have done to avoid the collision. The wife had then accompanied her husband to the hospital and immediately asked for a blood test report on Paul which was later submitted in evidence at the court. This showed Paul had not been drinking alcohol and, indeed, he happens to be a teetotaller.

The prosecution's arguments collapsed. Paul had won because his wife had realized that the quality of the documentary evidence you present is the vital element in a criminal case. Luckily, Paul had a wife who was up to the mark even though she was not a highly educated woman. The case also illustrated that the common belief that Thai courts are biased in favour of Thais is absolutely wrong. No Thai judge I have ever known was even remotely interested in the nationality of the persons arraigned before him. That's not how the Thai system works. Paul's experience also reflects that some marriages between foreigners and Thais work out just fine.

None the less, the golden rule is to avoid the Thai courts if at all possible.

Pattaya's Walking Street, the centre of adult evening entertainment, is the city's best known landmark. *Copyright: Pattaya Today.*

In uniform as the press officer for the Foreign Tourist Police Assistants. With me (right) is Dave Eke, a former security specialist. *Copyright: Author's collection.*

Colin Martin spent years in Thai jails for a murder he said he never committed.
Copyright: Andrew Drummond/Andrew Chant.

Michael Stacpoole (left) was the highest profile Brit I ever assisted in the Thai deportation process. *Copyright: Andrew Drummond/Andrew Chant.*
Paul Cryne (right) committed a murder whilst on overseas bail. *Copyright: Andrew Drummond/Andrew Chant.*

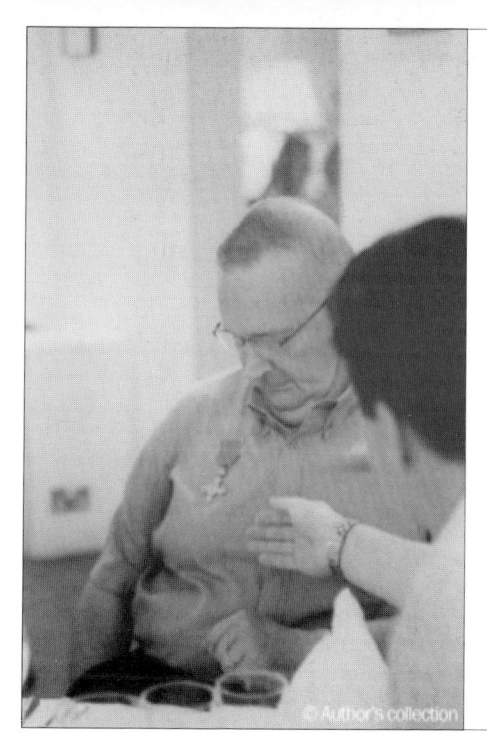

Having difficulty sticking the MBE onto my shirt at an embassy party in 2008. The award was mysteriously bestowed two years after being announced. *Copyright: Author's collection.*

With senior immigration police officers at the opening of the Chonburi Transnational Crimes Bureau. *Copyright: Author's collection.*

The doomed British consulate in Pattaya in a photo taken just before its final closure in late 2012. *Copyright: Pattaya Today.*

A boyish and somewhat camp Barry Kenyon in his proudest moment after gaining a first class honours degree in Latin, Greek and ancient history at Liverpool University. *Copyright: Author's collection.*

TWELVE: HELL WITH COLIN MARTIN

In the early days of my embassy tenure I was asked to visit any Irish nationals who found themselves in prison for a lengthy period in the Pattaya area. This was because the nearest Irish embassy was located in Kuala Lumpur, Malaysia, and a consulate had not been opened in Bangkok. Of course there is one there now, dealing mainly with passports and visas, although the overall directional control remains with the Irish embassy in Malaysia.

Colin Martin, an Irish welder with experience of well-paid jobs on oil rigs, has become famous since his release from a Thai jail in 2005. He has authored – I think there was a ghost writer involved – a best-selling book about his prison life Welcome to Hell, published by Maverick House, which has sold amazingly well in Europe, Australia, New Zealand and Thailand. It is still prominently displayed in the bookshops at Bangkok's principal international airport and many other places throughout the kingdom.

To say that Colin's story is a grim one would be serious understatement. He was the victim of a boiler-room scam, those often-elaborate conspiracies to defraud individuals of their cash or wealth. Bangkok, it's true to say, is an Asian centre for this particular activity and the scams are usually run by foreigners trying to trick other foreigners into parting with their bank details, investing in fake businesses or whatever. The journalist Andrew Drummond has many exposures of boiler-room scams on his blog site. I myself have experienced several attempts by phone and email to persuade me to release personal details which would enable scammers to decimate my personal finances. One of the give-away introductions is when you are asked, "How are you today sir?" The answer is to turn off the phone or to delete the message.

Unfortunately Colin had never heard of Andrew Drummond and was totally naïve about life in Bangkok as he freely admits in his book: he saw only hot weather, gorgeous girls and great food. In 1994 Colin saw a newspaper advertisement for a Bangkok based company, Offshore Construction Services (OCS), and was lured on a business trip from Europe to Bangkok where he was asked to source suitable foreign men to work on a nearby oil rig. After several meetings in a luxurious Bangkok office with officials of the totally fake company, Colin was persuaded that she should issue bonds to guarantee the workers and ended up paying a huge sum of money, namely US$264,000.

At first Colin wasn't suspicious. The office in question had 15 or so secretaries using computers or otherwise running a typical and bona fide business enterprise. The truth began to emerge after the OCS principal bank in the Polynesian islands proved to be a fake too, the luxurious office became suddenly empty and the conmen running the organization declined to answer their phones. Colin's spirits were raised momentarily when he did receive a communication from OCS but it was merely a card wishing him a Happy Christmas. He had been scammed out of a fortune.

Colin spent the next three years in Asia trying to find the foreign men who had cheated him. He was now unemployed, often destitute and also had a broken marriage on his hands back in Ireland. Colin's perseverance was truly amazing and he even married a local Thai woman Nanglung with whom he had a baby boy called Brendan. Eventually he found one of the men involved and obtained the address of another. After tricking the OCS managing director, New Zealand national Gerald O'Connor, into meeting him Colin ended up scuffling with the man's bodyguard, Brett Holdsworth, by the roadside. As they rolled down a grassy embankment Holdsworth ended up dead with knife wounds. It was 1997.

The nightmare then began in earnest. The police took the word of O'Connor and his wife that Colin was a murderer. He was allegedly beaten and tortured by police and forced to sign a false confession. He was then bundled off to Chonburi Central Prison, 65 kilometres from Pattaya, to await his trial for first-degree murder. He did not have sufficient resources to post bail and claimed that the Thai lawyer introduced by the Irish embassy was interested only in grabbing his fee. This lawyer did not even turn up at court on some occasions.

I first visited Colin in prison soon after his incarceration. I was absolutely stunned to see this gaunt yet steely 39-year old figure shuffling towards me in the visiting area. He was dragging with him the leg irons and manacles which shackled him. It was the practice in those days for the Thai prison authorities to confine prisoners on capital charges in this way until they were sentenced or acquitted by the provincial court. But my first impression of Colin was of a guy who could look after himself. Indeed he was a good boxer and, as revealed in his book, was not beyond punching and thumping people when he felt they had earned it.

Over the next few months his story was unfolded to me. He said that he wasn't carrying a weapon when Holdsworth died of knife wounds and fought him only in self-defence. In Colin's version, the bodyguard was the aggressor. There were certainly some odd features about the case. The knife allegedly used in the fatal stabbing was an old, rusty one which was never shown in court. Instead, the prosecution produced in evidence a black and white single-sheet photocopy of the weapon. Nor was any fingerprint evidence produced although the prosecutor did say there were traces of blood on the original (and unshown) knife, too small to identify the blood group. It was also strange that Holdsworth's body disappeared after the incident, seemingly dragged away by his associates, but later reappeared for a time. Officers from the New Zealand embassy in Bangkok actually claimed to have seen the body, but the results of an autopsy (if one was actually held) were never detailed in court. These irregularities would have been successfully challenged in a British criminal court.

When his trial was eventually held, with all the delays which are the hallmark of the Thai judicial system and expertly and even humorously detailed by Colin in Welcome to Hell, he was found guilty and sentenced to 20 years reduced by a third because he had originally signed a confession. The case was subsequently examined by both the appeals court and the supreme court but Colin spent eight years behind bars before being finally released early in early 2005. After several years he developed tuberculosis at Chonburi Central Prison and in 2001 was moved to a Bangkok prison with supposedly better medical facilities. One of Colin's principal worries was obviously money, always a much-needed item when you are locked up. His family did send cash at one point to post bail but Colin allowed his Thai wife to take control of it. She was a poor provincial girl with a family to support and the temptation to use most of it for her own needs proved to be too strong. Even so, when Chonburi Central Prison held its special, family open-days twice a year, Nanglung would turn up with Brendan. The happiest I ever saw Colin was when he was cuddling his young son.

In his book Colin scarcely refers to the Irish embassy and never to the British one. He always used to tell me he would use the opportunity of a book to illustrate their lack of care and competence. In fact he doesn't, perhaps because criticizing the diplomatic service might have turned the media spotlight away from his major conclusions about prison life. I learned from other prisoners that he felt I was pretty useless too on occasion. He would apparently say in the prison yard to fellow convicts every few weeks, "Fat Barry's overdue again!" I took the view that in his dire predicament harsh words were hardly surprising.

I did what I could, sending reports of each of my visits to the Irish embassy in Kuala Lumpur. I contacted Amnesty International and Prisoners Abroad on his behalf and smuggled out his letters to friends and supporters, paying for the postage out of my own pocket. Pattaya is a city with several Irish bars which I contacted with surprisingly good results. At least 75,000 baht (1,500 pounds) was raised and deposited over a long time in Colin's prison account to buy much-needed extra food and so-called comfort items such as a toothbrush, toothpaste, soap and the occasional blanket or towel. As time went on, well-wishers in Ireland sent parcels of food and the deputy governor told me that Colin received more postal items than any of the other foreigners incarcerated there.

When Colin was eventually sentenced in the provincial court, he had 30 days in which to send the appeal document to the higher court. Having no money to hire a lawyer, he wrote it out himself on scraps of paper covering the various legal points as best he could. Breaking British and Irish embassy rules, I took the scraps of paper on which he had made his points and paid for the translation into Thai from my own cash. Although it was obvious the very amateurish appeal would fail, and it did, I felt it was the appropriate thing to do. On several occasions I took piles of books donated by British residents of Pattaya for the prison library. Sometimes I had to act as censor because titles such as Clio The Whip Lady and Big Boobs in Bangkok would be frowned on by the prison authorities, especially if they were illustrated. One book which wrongly survived my sifting was the autobiography of Albert Pierrepoint, the most famous of British 20th century hangmen, an insensitive oversight on my part as Colin could theoretically have faced the death penalty. Shortly afterwards the Thai executioner Chavoret Jaruboon, who judicially shot 55 people in the back, published his own memoirs. In retirement, both Pierrepoint and Jaruboon came to the view that capital punishment achieves absolutely nothing in a society except to brutalise it further. It's sad that Thailand has not yet taken the decision to outlaw executions.

Colin frequently described in detail the inhuman treatment to which prisoners, both Thais and farangs, are subjected in the Thai prison system. I have no doubt that many of the sexual and violent horrors described by Colin in his book are true and similar claims have often been confirmed by other memoirs written by foreigners doomed to spend years as a guest of the Thai Department of Corrections. But I have to say that I personally never witnessed much horror, obviously because prison guards are on their best behaviour when embassy personnel are around. In the whole of my prison visiting over 12 years, I only once found a British prisoner who claimed he had been beaten – by another inmate as it happens. The overwhelming majority of complaints by British prisoners in general covered issues such as constant hunger pangs, itchy insect bites, cramped sleeping conditions on stone floors, almost non-existent medical facilities and being bored stiff as the TV, when not turned off, was invariably tuned to a Thai soap opera channel. But the brighter convicts, including Colin, learned to speak and even write the Thai language whilst teaching other prisoners and even the guards how to communicate in English. The key to survival in these places is to keep active as best you can.

Colin Martin survived as well as he did because of his iron will and never-flinching determination. Thus it's not totally surprising that according to press reports he returned to Bangkok months after his release in late 2005, not knowing if he would be refused entry at the airport as a blacklisted name according to media reports, to visit his former prisoner colleagues in Klong Prem Central Prison. He also met members of the Irish community in Bangkok at the Dubliner pub, who had supported him throughout, as well as looking into the question of his son Brendan joining him in Ireland. To my knowledge, he is the only European convicted of a capital crime in Thailand who even just once returned to the Land of Smiles. I imagine not many even wanted to.

There was a strange echo of the Colin Martin case in March 2013, several years after my retirement from the embassy, when a polite-sounding Thai woman requested a meeting with me. Her English was perfect. I met Khun Oy, now in her late 50s but still showing traces of her once-obvious beauty, at one of the many Starbucks coffee houses which litter Pattaya in the early 21st century. She told me that she had been working in 1994 for a secretarial and translation service which could be rented by the hour, the day or the week. Oy recalled being directed to a plush office in Bangkok where two New Zealand guys in striped suits told her to do some pretty meaningless work at a computer. She recalled the company name was Offshore Construction Services. She said she had read about Colin's story in the Thai press and had, more recently, read his book.

"You really ought to write a book too," she urged as she got up to meet her husband in the adjacent shopping mall.

THIRTEEN: THE POLITICIAN'S BAGMAN

The story of how Michael Stacpoole came to live in Pattaya and was subsequently deported for an immigration offence is a sad one. Not least because I got to like and know him, enough anyway to see his strengths and weaknesses. Michael was a close confidant of Jeffrey Archer – yes the Baron Archer of Weston-super-Mare – and had worked with him on business and fund-raising deals for many years. Apparently they first met in London in the 1960s when Michael was a high-profile PR consultant, working for a time for Wall's ice cream. Michael's other role seems to have been to be Lord Archer's drinking companion and escort to London clubs populated by ladies of easy virtue.

In September 1986 Lord Archer apparently picked up a London prostitute Monica Coghlan but was noticed by someone who had recently enjoyed the pleasure of her company. The stranger thought there might be financial mileage in reporting the matter to the British tabloid media, ever-ready to probe into the sex lives of the rich and famous. Lord Archer was a seasoned politician, a prolific author and for a time vice-chairman of the ruling Conservative party under Margaret Thatcher. Once he even campaigned to be the lord mayor of London.

Michael Stacpoole was told by Lord Archer to go to platform three of London's Victoria railway station and deliver a brown envelope to Ms Coghlan which contained 2,000 pounds or, according to Michael's much later account, a great deal more. But Sunday newspaper reporters were secretly taping and photographing the meeting. Ms Coghlan was a willing party to this undercover work and was allegedly paid 6,000 pounds by the News of the World. She said she needed the money to go abroad. Lord Archer always denied even meeting or knowing her but said he had received a request for help from her and decided to save her embarrassment.

Once the Monica Coghlan story broke later in 1986, Lord Archer paid his friend Michael a monthly allowance to leave the country and thus reduce the risk of his being subpoenaed to testify at any criminal proceedings. He spent eight months in Paris before returning to UK where the monthly payments continued, a total of about 40,000 pounds. He was certainly a danger to his boss as he knew about the novelist's infidelities, affairs and consorting with prostitutes. Lord Archer wanted to sue the Press for libel.

But Lord Archer won his legal battles with the tabloid press in 1987 and Michael was never called to the Old Bailey as a witness. Lord Archer and his lawyers persuaded the jury that he was a faithful husband and that the meeting with the prostitute never took place. The News of the World settled out of court allegedly for 20,000 pounds. But the Daily Star, which had gone much further in its allegations of deviant sex acts, found itself having to pay 500,000 pounds damages, then a record in a libel trial, as well as being lumbered with legal costs amounting to an even higher sum. Michael was bitter that his years of loyalty to Lord Archer were rewarded by what he saw as a paltry reward.

Post-trial, Lord Archer then arranged for Michael to get a job with a reclusive American millionaire, but the arrangements did not work out. At one point Michael had a worryingly huge mortgage on a house in Florida but appears to have reached some kind of financial agreement with the recluse. His immediate future after that is still unclear but he later told me that he ran a club in Belgium for two years before heading to Pattaya. This makes some sense as I recall from his passport that he was born in the West Flanders city of Ostend in the late 1930s.

I first met Michael Stacpoole in 1999 when he turned up at Pattaya bridge club which I was running at the time. "I'm no expert he told me, "but I enjoy a friendly game of cards."

Michael struggled quite a lot with some of the personalities at the club who were keen on a most competitive game. He was asked by a particularly domineering member, "Do you use in your bidding system British Acol or American five cards majors?" to which he replied nonchalantly "Well, it depends on whether I have had a drink or not." Michael often displayed an effective way of reducing tension when the odds were stacked against him.

At the time Michael was in his early 60s, with a shock of white hair and a very expensive-looking motorbike. A former public schoolboy, he was suave and sophisticated but with a tart wit when the occasion demanded it. He took criticism at the bridge table in good part but knew how to put people in their place if really necessary. He signed in at the bridge club under his real name, but neither I nor any other members realized who he was. In those days Pattaya was a something of a media backwater. British newspapers were rarely seen in the resort and the internet was in its infancy. It was well-nigh impossible at the time for a foreigner to have a mobile phone in his or her own name. Of course, it's a very different situation today.

At the time I was holding informal bridge sessions at my home on Thursday evenings to maintain interest in the club which met only once-weekly on a Monday afternoon. I invited Michael on several occasions and he was a popular figure, always pleasant and polite, regularly bringing a bottle of spirits to share, showing an interest in the others present and recognizing that he was not the world's gift to contract bridge. He struck me too as very even-tempered. On one unfortunate evening his expensive motorbike was stolen from outside my house.

"Well I'll just get another one," he said nonchalantly.

He was occasionally asked what was his career background and usually replied that he had been a marketing or public relations consultant in Europe and in the United States. But he mentioned neither his family nor Lord Archer.

In May 2000 I was telephoned by Michael to explain he had suffered a slight stroke which explained his absence from the bridge club. There was limited paralysis in his limbs and he had some trouble remembering things. He asked me to visit him on a confidential matter at his home in Pattaya which turned out to be a cottage hidden from the world down a long, winding road in a rural district. Greeting me with a walking stick and apologizing that the door bell didn't work, he commented that he always knew when someone was arriving as the cow in an adjacent field always mooed obligingly.

The confidential matter turned out to be his 10-year, expiring British passport which urgently needed replacing. Michael did not know where to get the forms or what to do. I said this was no problem as I could easily provide the forms and give him the necessary assistance.

It was at this meeting that Michael said he had best "come clean". After clarifying that I had no prior knowledge of him, he gave me a potted history of the Lord Archer affair which put all the blame on the well-known novelist and politician. Michael claimed he had been promised he would receive half of the huge libel award from the Daily Star and not the measly 40,000 pounds which in any case had been drip-fed to him over months.

He added that he had been visited at his Pattaya home earlier in 1999 by Scotland Yard detectives following the disclosure in the UK media that he had allegedly been paid-off by Lord Archer. Michael clarified that he wanted me to know his saga in outline, not because of my involvement in the embassy, but in case I did not want him playing bridge at my home. I replied this was no certainly no problem as one of the other regulars on a Thursday night claimed he was wanted in Switzerland for a bank robbery. In Pattaya you have to be broad-minded, we both agreed.

In August 2000 I was contacted by the Bangkok Hospital Pattaya to say that a British man had been badly injured in a motorcycle accident and was in the intensive care unit. It was

Michael Stacpoole. He had head injuries and a fractured shoulder but his life was not in danger. How Michael paid the bill I'm not sure as the bursar said that a third party had funded both the operations and the convalescence. I assumed it was his family. However, I do remember Michael saying that the hospital bills had made him a much poorer man.

Some months later Bangkok-based investigative journalist Andrew Drummond phoned me to say that he had tracked down Stacpoole whose evidence was important because of tales circulating in London that Lord Archer had committed perjury in the 1987 Daily Star trial. In the event Michael sold his story to the Mail on Sunday for an undisclosed fee. In due course Lord Archer was sent to prison for two years (2001-2003) for perjury although, once again, Michael Stacpoole was not called as a witness. When news of Michael's notoriety reached the ears of the embassy in Bangkok, I received a phone call to the effect that the ambassador was none-too-pleased that his Pattaya diplomatic representative had been entertaining at home controversial British figures with an unsavoury media profile and that I would hear from the "political section of the embassy" in due course. I imagined that this Gestapo-sounding body would be investigating whether I should receive the chop. In the event I heard nothing further about the matter.

Michael stopped playing bridge, for whatever reason, and enjoyed the night-life of Pattaya presumably funded by his disclosures to the Mail on Sunday. I saw him occasionally in supermarkets or whilst he was parking his motorbike on the roadside. But he appeared to be going downhill, unshaven and bedraggled in appearance. His latest motorbike, I noticed, was a very cheap, rented one. It was also plain to see that there were adverse consequences on his health from the stroke and the serious traffic accident. Some days he looked like a tramp.

In early 2003 I was contacted by a duty officer at Pattaya police station to say that a British man was asking for me in the holding cells. Michael Stacpoole had been arrested for overstaying his visa by several months. He told me from behind the grille that he had totally run of money but gave me the telephone number of a family member in the Channel Islands. I visited his last known rented address, a very humble town-house in a remote district of Naklua, where the woman owner told me that Michael had not paid his rent for many weeks and that, as a result, she had reported him for an overstay visa. This, by the way, is a not uncommon strategy when Thai landlords want to get rid of non-paying tenants who lack the resources to leave the country to renew their paperwork. It's a short-cut which frees up your accommodation for re-letting straight away.

The Thais are generally lenient when it comes to matters of overstay. Offenders can usually pay the fine of 500 baht (10 pounds) a day up to a maximum of 20,000 baht (400 pounds) and be allowed to leave the country unhindered. But if you can't pay, or if you are arrested first, then it's an automatic procedure to be taken to court and subsequently deported at your own expense. There is no bail for overstay offenders so the guilty have to remain in jail until somebody, anybody, comes up with the cash to pay for the air ticket back to the country of origin: the UK in the case of Michael.

In the event, Michael's relative provided the necessary funds very quickly through a Thai intermediary in Pattaya. I was given to understand that Michael was something of a family problem. He cut a forlorn figure in the Pattaya police cells – no possessions, no money, not even a change of clothing. But he remained amazingly cheerful, passing the time of day with the colourful assembly of the wicked and the unfortunate who are forced to spend time there.

I brought him the usual luxuries including door-stop sandwiches, a bar of soap, a towel, and a new T-shirt and pair of shorts.

"It's not too bad in here old boy," he said, "a transvestite cut my toe nails this morning for half a Mars bar. I never knew they had a heart."

But he was clearly anxious to know how long he would remain in this particular hell-hole. In fact, because of his relative's generosity, we were able to grease the necessary palms to speed up the procedure, clear the vast volume of paperwork which accompanies these proceedings and purchase the ticket. The whole business took just about a week. I last saw Michael Stacpoole peering out of the back of a police van with bloodshot and bleary eyes on his way to Bangkok airport. He said he would be back in Thailand within a few months to resume the high life.

Of course, he never did return.

FOURTEEN: THE CONTRACT KILLER

In October 2003 the local Pattaya media reported the murder of Robert Henry, a 42-year old Cardiff-born expat who ran the Skydive bar in Pattaya's infamous street Soi Yodsak, commonly known as Sexy Soi Six. Neighbours told investigators the bar was a scene of frequent loud arguments which sometimes spilled out into the street. Henry had previously run Siam Air Sport, a skydiving operation which collapsed when its sole plane crashed on take-off at a Pattaya air strip injuring the eight or so passengers and crew inside. He was also known locally as a boxing promoter who arranged for Thais to fight in British stadiums, especially in the Coventry area where he had lived.

Henry had been found face-down in a swampy Jomtien canal with six bullets fired from an automatic pistol inside him. There were motorbike tracks at the scene leading away from the body. Investigators in the case soon decided that the murder was linked to Siam Air Sport saying that the Henry had likely argued with other shareholders and that there had been wrangling over the distribution of the insurance company pay-out after the crash at the air strip in which, freak accident that it was, nobody had been killed. Henry's wife Khun Wilai claimed that her husband had been kidnapped before being murdered by a greedy business associate.

Initially police issued a warrant for the arrest of former SAS soldier Ron Loveridge, also from Coventry and the founder of Siam Air Sport, but he quickly contacted police and was released without charge. He had been on a visa run to Cambodia when the murder had occurred. Investigators then turned their attention to Paul Cryne, born in Manchester and then in his early sixties, as they had found blood on the back seat of Cryne's BMW car which police said he had sent to have stripped, re-upholstered and re-sprayed at a Naklua garage soon after the murder.

Police then arrested Paul Cryne at a local garage and charged him with first-degree murder. He was detained in Pattaya Remand Prison on the outskirts of the city. It was here that I first met him as a witness for the interviewing Thai police officer and advisor to Cryne in what could become a capital case warranting the death penalty. He denied the charge, agreeing that he worked with Robert Henry on several projects but had absolutely no reason to murder him. He pointed out that Henry's Thai wife Wilai stood to inherit the cash and wealth which the deceased possessed in Thailand.

Cryne stressed that his job in Thailand was importing expensive-looking second-hand cars and renovating them for resale. Therefore, he said, the work being done on the BMW was routine and nothing out of the ordinary. It was purely a coincidence that the work was being carried out shortly after Henry's body was discovered. As regards the blood on the back seat, this was easily explained. It belonged to his dog which had been fighting with another dog and had sought refuge in the car. He admitted that Henry had taken a few rides in the BMW in the front passenger seat but not on the day of the shooting.

I ascertained at the prison that Cryne did not have enough money to post bail or to hire a lawyer. However he provided a couple of phone numbers of friends who might be willing to help out. After several weeks, an American acquaintance of his did indeed get him released and even put up a small sum to obtain some legal advice. The bailed Brit disappeared to Koh Chang, an island of Trat province several hours travelling from Pattaya. Here he lived with his Thai girlfriend in humble surroundings by the tropical rain forests and the exotic coral reefs. From time to time he would visit Pattaya and we would usually have a coffee or an orange juice. He was strictly teetotal.

It took nearly two years for the murder case to be heard at Pattaya court. Several times the judge postponed the proceedings because key prosecution witnesses, including Henry's Thai wife Wilai and also a forensics expert, failed to turn up. Wilai never did show as a matter of fact. Finally, in 2005, Cryne was found not guilty but any celebrations were short-lived as the prosecution decided to appeal purely on the DNA evidence of the blood on the back seat of the BMW. Although attempts had been made to wipe or scrub the blood away, and only traces remained, forensic scientists still believed there was a case to answer linking Cryne to Henry's death.

Luckily for Cryne, another friend of his managed successfully to re-apply for a second bail pending consideration by the appeal court, a process we knew would take at least another two years.

The man from Manchester resumed his quiet existence on Koh Chang until one day in late 2007 he requested an urgent meeting with me in Pattaya. He explained that he was extremely short of cash but had been offered a six-month job on an oil rig in the North Sea which he wished to accept provided he could obtain the permission of the court. If not, he would be refused exit at Thai airports and land crossings.

It may seem astonishing that an alleged foreign murderer in Thailand would be allowed to leave the country, promising to come back after six months to continue waiting for the appeal court judgment. A Thai lawyer agreed to submit an application for "overseas bail" on the grounds that the defendant needed to make some money in order to survive. The application also covered the points that Cryne was a lifeguard and swimming champion, meriting a mention in the Guinness Book of Records for alleged scuba-related achievements, had been injured in a sea accident in the Maldives and had done many good works in Thailand, including teaching locals the arts of diving and snorkelling for free. Of course he promised in writing he would return to the Land of Smiles at the expiry of the North Sea work contract.

Much to my astonishment and, I think, that of Cryne and the submitting lawyer, the request was granted. Actually such requests are often made in long drawn-out cases and sometimes agreed. I recall another case where a ganja smuggler was given leave to go to Laos to work on a chicken farm collecting eggs and was never seen again from that day to this. The seemingly generous policy by the courts is partly a recognition that the Thai judicial system is painfully slow and partly a secret hope, in my opinion, that the defendant will abscond for good and thus save the Thai courts a great deal of time, effort and money. However, there was a hidden reason why Cryne wanted to get out of Thailand and go, not to Denmark, but to the UK. Interestingly, the ticket he showed at Bangkok international airport was allegedly for London (not Copenhagen) but this failed to alert the immigration authorities.

Paul Cryne believed that he would get away with the perfect murder. He was paid 30,000 pounds by Graham Birchwood to murder 52-year old Sharon Birchwood at her bungalow in Ashtead, Surrey, in December 2007. Graham Birchwood stood to gain a 475,000 pounds pot-of-gold from the will of his former wife who had remained devoted to him despite their divorce in 1989. He had gone on to marry his secretary with whom he had two children. Birchwood had accumulated a lot of debts and was facing bankruptcy. Realising that he would fall under suspicion if his former wife was murdered, he needed a hit-man who could then disappear without even attracting the attention of the British police. Birchwood by the way is now serving a long prison sentence for conspiracy to murder.

Sharon Birchwood, who had a serious neurological disease, was strangled in her home on her bed and left cruelly trussed-up with parcel tape and electrical cord. Thinking he was in the clear, Cryne then flew back to Bangkok in fulfilment of the terms of his overseas bail permission from the Thai court. But perfect murders are notoriously hard to perform. DNA at the scene of the crime matched that on a cup at Birchwood's mother's house where Cryne had briefly stayed during his recent sojourn. There was also fingerprint evidence on police files linking him to a wholly separate crime in 1972. Back in Thailand, he appeared fresh and confident.

He had money in his pocket and recounted a totally fictional story of how he had saved a man's life in an accident on the oil rig in the North Sea. He resumed his life of retirement on Koh Chang pointing out that it was a much better place than Pattaya which was full of villains and criminals. Meanwhile the Surrey police had tracked down a wanted man to Thailand and two officers were in Pattaya on a mission to obtain further evidence if they could. I agreed to meet the policemen.

I do not feel especially proud that I agreed to have lunch with Paul Cryne specifically in order for the British cops, hidden nearby, secretly to take DNA evidence from the cutlery and glasses he used during the meal. It seemed the right thing to do especially as the DNA and fingerprint evidence against him was already formidable. I might add that the police photographs of Sharon Birchwood's corpse were amongst the most gruesome I ever saw. She had obviously died in awful terror and agony.

I did receive verbal approval from my immediate consular superior in Bangkok but I also got a strong ticking-off from the consul-in-charge Gordon MacCleod. I was told that Gordon, who died suddenly in 2010 following a tragic accident in the embassy grounds, made a mental note that I had exceeded my responsibilities. Actually what I did is described in legal circles as Queen's Business (or so I was informed) which in frank terms means that governmental officials are permitted to carry out special instructions on Her Majesty's service notwithstanding other regulations. Gordon was not exactly delighted when I mentioned this to him.

In 2009 the Thai police arrested Cryne at his Ko Chang home and a long period of wrangling occurred as the British police tried to extradite him whilst the Thai authorities pointed out that they were waiting for the appeal court ruling in the case of Robert Henry's murder of 2003. But some sort of agreement was worked out and Paul Cryne, still claiming he was innocent of any and all murders, was extradited back to England by UK police officers late in 2009. I thought that was probably my last connection with the Paul Cryne case. But I was wrong.

The prosecution in UK wanted three witnesses from the British embassy in Bangkok to attend the murder trial at the Old Bailey in 2010, namely two Bangkok-based consular officers and myself. All of us had already given detailed statements to the Surrey police. We all objected that we could not spare the time and I think we all realized we were minor witnesses in the saga as a whole. In the end it was agreed that we could give our evidence one-by-one by video link at the Bangkok embassy, an increasingly commonly-used technology, and special equipment was used to connect us to the Old Bailey at the appropriate moment. Of course, our scheduled time in the afternoon, by the UK clock, meant it was already evening in Thailand.

I was expecting a grilling but nothing of that sort happened in my half-hour testimony. The prosecution spent several minutes asking me about how I took notes when visiting prisoners and also about the process by which I sent on the reports. By email to my superiors of course! I could only conclude that embassy practices were being checked for discrepancies as we gave our evidence in turn and without anyone else in the room. The defence barrister probed whether Cryne had ever talked about his alleged hit-man activities but I replied in the negative, adding that if Cryne had indeed made a career out of this activity it had not been successful as he was nearly always desperately short of cash. The judge intervened at one point to ask if my job entailed meeting a lot of villains. Yes my lud!

In the event Cryne was found guilty by a jury of his peers for the murder of Sharon Birchwood and judge Jeremy Roberts said he must serve at least 28 and a half years. "You may well spend the rest of your life behind bars. If you do, I am afraid that will be the consequence of your own actions."

Cryne did not appeal the sentence although he had originally pleaded not guilty and even produced a witness who had allegedly seen Sharon Birchwood in a supermarket after she had supposedly been strangled. Some weeks later I received a letter of commendation from the Surrey police. By this time my embassy contract had expired and I was no longer Her Majesty's Pattaya representative in Sin City. Whoever killed Robert Henry is not publicly known to this day.

FIFTEEN: MBE AND PEDOPHILIA

As the years went by, the amount of consular work in Pattaya zoomed upwards. That was not only because holidaying and expat Brits were in trouble. There was also a growing number of requests for notarial services, especially income confirmation letters for the local immigration bureau. Increasing numbers of Brits over 50 years of age on long-term visas needed an embassy-signed letter detailing that their income, usually pensions originating in UK, was worth at least 800,000 baht (around 16,000 pounds) on an annual basis. Many were complaining that they had to make a special journey to the embassy in Bangkok, some 120 kilometres away, to obtain the letter or risk the vagaries of the Thai postal system. Given the large British expat population in Pattaya, the embassy seemed inclined to appease them.

In 2004 I was given an official receipt book and an embassy ink stamp to enable me to issue these highly-valued letters locally. In good months I took four thousand pounds or more without any security precautions or additional personnel. Because I lacked an office and worked from my home which was a private address,

I decided to use as a base a coffee shop in the car park of the Pattaya immigration bureau, actually located in Jomtien. The cafe proprietors were more than happy with this arrangement as it boosted their business by providing an additional commercial opportunity on their premises as visitor numbers increased. This was a highly unusual facility for any British embassy to offer, equalled perhaps only by a former honorary consul in Spain who advertised that he would be available at certain times round the swimming pool of his favourite five star hotel unless it happened to be raining or was windy. Apparently you were meant to look for the guy in the purple swimming trunks wearing a floral hat. You were also advised to bring a plastic cover to protect your documents lest they became splashed by the hotel revellers.

The "coffee shop experiment", as it was called, in fact lasted until the beginning of 2009. The opening time was initially limited to just one hour each morning (excluding weekends and holidays) although this was extended after I was given a part-time Thai assistant in 2007. Each morning up to 15 Brits would visit the coffee shop for any number of reasons: obtaining an income letter for immigration, enquiring about passport renewals, wanting information about a UK visa for a Thai girlfriend and even complaining about the price of mangoes in the supermarket. I also dealt with down-and-outs openly wondering how they could go back to England without any money, bereaved parents of young men who had been killed in road accidents and the occasional bipolar individual, without medication for whatever reason, believing he was being followed by malevolent strangers wherever he went. You mention it. We experienced it. There was even one guy who regularly slept under cars in the neighbourhood and used to walk up and down mimicking Boris Karloff's interpretation of the Frankenstein monster with the outstretched arms. He explained that "wine is good, but fire no good", an expression borrowed from the 1931 movie.

In 2005 I received a phone call from the then ambassador David Fall to inform me that my status had been upgraded from consular correspondent to honorary consul. This came after a long bureaucratic exercise in which I had filled in countless forms about my work and had been subject to high-level security clearance back in the UK. The promotion came with a small tax-free gratuity of 2,300 pounds a year, the maximum allowed under the rules, as well as car fuel and allied expenses. In practical terms the adoption of the term honorary consul meant very little and my duties remained pretty much as they had been previously. In the ensuing publicity, the website thaivisa.com seemed to confuse the title honorary consul with being made a knight of the realm and irritatingly used the title Sir Barry Kenyon. Not everything you read on the internet is true.

The following year, 2006, I was awarded MBE (Member of the British Empire) in the summer announcements which are issued in the name of the Queen Elizabeth. It was then unusual for serving members of the Bangkok embassy to be awarded this particular medal, the last time apparently being some nine years previously when a senior official was rewarded after her stalwart work with a British woman who was sentenced to death in Thailand, but later pardoned, after admitting drugs charges. My award was less spectacularly granted for general services to the British community in Thailand. It's fair to say I had never sought a 'gong', as these honours are nicknamed, as I have always been dubious about the system in principle. However I accepted in good grace as a token of respect to the ambassador David Fall, far and away the most competent of any I encountered and one of the very few who was more concerned with the efficiency of the service than with promoting his own ego, and because it would have seemed churlish on my part to behave otherwise. I took some comfort from the fact that in the same list that summer another ageing Liverpudlian also received the MBE. She had worked in the same fish and chip shop since before the Second World War and was a devoted lollypoplady at the crossing outside a Merseyside junior school.

What I did not realize at the time was that the honours list was always scrutinized carefully by reporters of the so-called gutter press in UK. In September of 2006 I suddenly started receiving nasty SMS messages on my mobile phone.

They were both threatening and disgusting in their explicitness and claimed that I was taking underage boys to my home for illegal sexual activity. I did not take much notice of the nuisance calls at the time, assuming that they originated with some angry Brit dissatisfied with an embassy service he had tried to use. It was obvious in a role like mine that universal popularity was neither feasible nor even desirable. Some of the messages suggested I should reply to the anonymous critic, but I declined. Silence is often a good policy in difficult circumstances. At the time I was more concerned with painful attacks of gout in my left foot than with the idle chitchat of some malcontent.

Then the nasty messages suddenly stopped. Two weeks later I received a phone call from a guy who was well-known as an investigative journalist from London who specialized in sex cases, by name Roger Insall. Actually he spent quite a lot of time in Thailand and there were rumours he was connected to a Bangkok massage parlour. Pattaya was a favourite port of call and he had a number of exposure pelts under his belt by this time including a dubious attempt to incriminate Father Ray Brennan of the Pattaya orphanage in a sex scandal. The priest, who was accused of allowing foreign pedophiles to gain access to youngsters, suffered a fatal heart attack within a year doubtless brought on by the unlikely suggestions. Now there is certainly a defence of sex investigators for newspapers such as The News of the World (now defunct of course). They do uncover matters which are most certainly in the public interest. A necessary evil you might say. The problem is that they are sometimes wrong in their assumptions, insinuations and accusations.

In all I received four phone calls from Mr Insall in Thailand over a period of about a week. He started off by trying to suggest I was a good friend of a pedophile who had recently committed suicide in Pattaya. This was actually untrue. I had merely visited this guy for the first time in the police cells as a professional duty when he was first arrested. I was later summoned by the police to his abode when he was found by a neighbour with a plastic bag over his head and a hastily-drunk whisky bottle at his side. Roger Insall then changed tack suggested that I was a disgrace to the honours system as he had evidence that young Thai boys were visiting me at home. When I asked what this evidence was, he replied that an early-teen prostitute in one of Pattaya's gay bars could describe the inside of my house and even my bedroom. Roger tried very hard to coerce me into meeting him for a chat and a drink on the basis that I could well convince him that the accusations were wrong. However I knew enough about sex journalists of the tabloid press in London to appreciate that such a meeting would be inevitably disastrous from my point of view. Whatever I said would be twisted and turned to make a front-page story along the lines of "Honourable Pattaya vice consul exposed!" I'm no Max Mosley and don't have the funds to sue influential newspapers for printing nonsense.

Roger also revealed he knew I was gay, as if this was some kind of state secret. But I had worked in gay rights in Manchester in the 1970s, was a regular columnist under my own name for the newspaper Gay News and obviously had many gay friends in Pattaya. I was even a committee member of the Pattaya Gay Pride fund-raising organization for aids-related charities. However the attack was not yet suspended. The next phone call was from Mazher Mahmood, also known as the Fake Sheik, from his journalist's office in London. He began shouting at me down the phone that undercover reporters had been in Pattaya for six weeks and had clear photographic evidence that I was a frequent customer in sex bars catering for pedophiles picking up youngsters in the Sunee Plaza district of Pattaya.

I knew that this guy specialized in exposing the rich and the famous so, in a bizarre sense, I felt flattered to be paid such attention by the master who has put at least 100 major criminals behind bars. However, I decided to cut the conversation short by terminating the call. In any case I was driving to the local vet at the time as the family cat needed its annual injections. It's not easy driving a car in Pattaya with a struggling feline in one hand and a prominent investigator in the other vying for your attention at the same time. Let's be clear: it's no fun having these guys on your back. Immediately the phone calls started, I wrote a round-robin email to about 20 officers in the embassy, including the ambassador, to explain the nature of the harassment.

David Fall offered his full support and even set up an informal committee of three in the embassy to monitor the matter. He also said he would notify the Foreign Office staff in London to contact various Sunday tabloids to ascertain what they trying to do. Actually I was quite overcome by the support I received from many consular officers in Bangkok, both foreign and Thai, especially the women. Interestingly, one of the few who did not rally to the cause was a closet gay working in the Bangkok embassy who had once fled when we accidentally met in a Bangkok gay bar. One of the positive results of this bizarre story is that he came out of the closet later to friends, family and employer.

The Foreign Office in London duly contacted the tabloid and discovered that the News of the World was indeed contemplating a story which might be in next week's issue. But next week came and went and absolutely nothing appeared. Further official contacts with the newspaper produced the same vague threat for the future. Nobody knew what exactly I was accused of. It was like being in a criminal court and not knowing the charges. I also contacted well-connected, Bangkok-based investigative journalist Andrew Drummond who proved to be very helpful. He revealed there had been rumours circulating in Fleet Street about a pedophile working for the British embassy in Pattaya and that the News of the World was the only newspaper rich enough to send out investigators to learn the hoped-for details. Andrew said he would contact appropriate editors to point out that the evidence linking Barry Kenyon to personal pedophile activity was likely to be on the sparse side. And that was that. No newspaper article ever appeared. A journalist friend in London told me the News of the World did have a photo of me emerging from a semi-gay pub in Pattaya which was having its weekly quiz night. Given that I was the question setter for the Pattaya pub quiz league at the time – and still am – that's hardly surprising. Someone else contacted me to suggest that a certain London editor of a tabloid newspaper recognized she might stir a hornet's nest as I would be likely to start screaming about lies, harassment and defamation. Too true I would.

Of course some people say there's no smoke without fire. There was one interesting consequence connecting the MBE and the sex allegations which seems to bear out the point. When I was first told of the MBE, weeks before the tabloid harassment, I mentioned that I would not be going to Buckingham Palace to receive the medal. The reason was very simple. I would only travel by air such a long distance in woefully expensive business class, but there was no subsidy from official sources and I had no other reason to visit UK at the time.

The alternative was to receive the medal from the ambassador here in Thailand. No problem. So I waited and waited and waited. And then waited some more. Clearly, I thought, somebody high-up in the diplomatic world was playing the game of ensuring there was no delayed and ghastly exposure in the Sunday press after all.

It was a full two years after the events described above before I received an invitation in 2008 to receive the MBE from the next ambassador, Quinton Quayle, who became famous for surprisingly abandoning his diplomatic career in 2010 to take up an appointment in international, alcoholic beverages.

Quinton, a fluent Thai speaker by the way, was also involved in an unfortunate debacle when the BBC reported that a former British ambassador to Thailand in the 1960s, Anthony Rumbold, had once said that the Thais had no culture worth speaking of and were motivated only by sex. Quinton was left to defend Amazing Thailand which he did with aplomb I have to say, pointing out the country had changed greatly in 40 years.

This frank criticism by former ambassador Rumbold was revealed after the BBC used the freedom of information legislation to obtain dispatches from ambassadors for its radio series Parting Shots. Some were released under the 30-year rule of the national archives. These dispatches are a treasure trove of supposedly secret opinions which are now seeing the light of day. I particularly liked the remarks of David Gore-Booth, the son of a diplomat, who wrote, "One of the great failures of the diplomatic service has been its inability to cast off its image as bowler-hatted, pin-striped and chinless, with a fondness for champagne."

I like to think I played a role in shaking off that image although my fondness for champagne remains intact.

SIXTEEN: READ ALL ABOUT IT

The Pattaya media have had a bad press. The English-speaking local newspapers are attacked on Thai blog sites because they don't report scandals and corruption, preferring to stick to small court cases, glorification of City Hall officials and lots of personal photos to puff up the self-importance of the farang media moguls. Some say the local TV stations and on-line news outlets are no better, concentrating on minor crimes graphically illustrated by blurred photographs of severed limbs in road accidents and wretched suicides hanging from a tree. Still, repeated sociological research has shown that shocks and bad news, especially with photos, sell the media even though the readers and viewers are too shy to admit so.

Of course, it's not only in Pattaya. If you look at provincial media throughout the Asian continent you will discover that their political significance is on a scale from almost zero to total zero. Come to that, it can be questioned whether or not the British local media are much different. I still visit on-line The Colne Times and the Liverpool Echo and find the same diet I remember as a child: local crime, weddings and what's on at the local cinema or TV. Everything has to be local, parochial even. It's said that when a Lancashire evening paper reported the sinking of the Titanic in 1912, it used as a headline "Blackburn man hurts arm in sea accident".

The doyen of the Pattaya print media is the weekly Pattaya Mail whose first printing was in 1993. It's a staid publication, particularly strong on local sports, well supported by advertisers and commonly believed to be read by Pattaya's expat elite except that nobody is quite sure who they are. One of its best columnists, dating back to the 1990s, is Dr Iain Corness who triples-up as an agony columnist, a restaurant reviewer and a motor racing correspondent. He is also the author of a witty literary insight into Thai life seen through foreign eyes entitled Farang. He is separately a medical consultant at the Bangkok Hospital Pattaya.

For some years in the 1990s I wrote anonymously a column Grapevine in Pattaya Mail which covered the more unusual aspects of Pattaya life including the bouncing rhinos of the local zoo, the friendly ghosts of Naklua sea front and police raids on a local gay bar with the unusual title Vaseline for Life. I stopped soon after being recruited by the British embassy. I was asked by the consul of the time, "Who writes this crap?" Dunno sir! I still maintain a loose contact with Pattaya Mail and am moved to write a reader's letter from time to time when arrant nonsense appears in Postbag.

In 2001 I happened to pick up a copy of the fortnightly Pattaya Today which I noticed was full of spelling and printing errors.

One of the most glaring was a misspelling of the name of A.J.P. Taylor, the famous "historian", which had come out as "shitorian" and was presumably an unintended criticism of the great researcher and lecturer. With nothing better to do whilst waiting for a plane at Bangkok international airport, I went through the entire publication with a red-ink pen and, in due course, handed it in at the newspaper's Pattaya office with a curt note telling the editor where to go. The then owner, a Thai lady by the name of Visa Chimdee, immediately phoned me and offered me a job which later resulted in my appointment as deputy editor until she sold the business in 2009. I might be the only person in the whole global history of the media who obtained a well-paid job after rubbishing the product.

Pattaya Today boomed, I have to admit, and was the first Pattaya publication to produce its own property supplement, a tradition which continues to this day. Much of the marketing was done by Visa's husband Chris who sadly died of cancer in 2007. We tried to develop a different image from that of Pattaya Mail, more chatty and diverse in content, which worked surprisingly well for many years. Since my time, the paper has changed ownership twice and currently appears in three discrete and colourful sections: news, lifestyle and business/property. I still write profiles and columns on a free-lance basis. The biggest scoop Pattaya Today ever had was in 2006 when the immigration bureau nationally introduced many changes to the visa rules for foreigners. I offered on-line assistance to people not clear about their personal position and in two short weeks replied to over 950 enquiries from all over the world. These days, there would be many legal experts and blog sites to answer the on-line hunger for correct information. But not in 2006, just a few short years ago.

One incident in 2008 caused an international outcry. It was April 1, April Fools' Day, and we decided to run a spoof story about the last survivor of the Titanic dying at the age of 98 after a short illness in her home near Jomtien beach. A heart-rending tale was told of how this infant from Hungary (there were many steerage passengers from eastern Europe) was thrown into a lifeboat at the last minute when her mother had apparently got lost on the sloping boat deck. The small girl's arm had been damaged in the fall. She had been raised by foster parents in the United States and later married a Thai man which explained how she ended up in the Pattaya area. Given the rock-solid interest in the Titanic disaster, especially in UK and US, we were inundated with requests and demands for further information and clarification as the item also appeared in the newspaper's on-line edition. We even had an email from the nursing home in Southampton, where the true last survivor of the Titanic, Milvina Dean, was still living, asking if we could help financially to contribute to her private medical care following a broken hip. It was a tactless April Fools' Day joke on my part and one I regretted.

Of course, there are many other local media including the weekly newspaper Pattaya People (a vanity press publication par excellence), the internet news channels Pattaya One and Pattaya Daily News, several radio and TV stations, blog sites galore including the very popular Thaivisa.com (based in Bangkok) and several magazines covering the issues of property or lifestyle or both. And that total is just for the English language publications and omitting those that have ceased publication such as the totally unremarkable print newspaper Pattaya Times which in its latter months appeared irregularly and was nicknamed by a clerk at the printing works Pattaya Sometimes. It's something of a paradox that Pattaya has so much English media when the actual number of tourists and expats in the resort who use English as a first language may be actually be declining as Pattaya turns increasingly to Asia for its tourist catchment. The print media remains surprisingly strong in Pattaya in popularity terms, perhaps reflecting the fact that many first-language English speakers are older and less reliant on the newfangled social media. This, of course, will likely change in the years ahead.

And then there's Andrew Drummond whose beady eye on his alternative news internet site has been watching Pattaya for 20 years. He's an independent journalist based in Bangkok but in fact covers the whole of south east Asia. A former Fleet Street reporter of wide experience, he is as you might expect diligent, shrewd and durably controversial. Much of his work has won acclaim including his investigations into racism and fascism in Europe which led to his being awarded the Maurice Ludmer memorial prize and his prompt coverage of breaking-news such as the 2004 Asian tsunami, the Bali bombings and the bird flu crisis. He is especially good at tracking people down and, with photographer Andrew Chant, found sex-offender Garry Glitter at a Vietnamese beach resort.

Early on, I was told by the embassy to give a wide berth to Andrew Drummond. "He's not on our side you see," was the summary judgment of one senior official. But that caution misunderstands what the journalist is doing. Andrew exposes what he knows to be wrong. On his website, he'll attack embassy personnel, business personalities, and frauds and fakers of all kinds if the story needs telling and provided he has documentary evidence to back up his claims. He is perhaps the only true investigative journalist in Thailand or even throughout all Asia. Yes he can be wrong. He once had a hunch I was acting unprofessionally and in a biased way regarding the case of a British man from Halifax imprisoned for drugs, but apologized after he found out the truth. In 2011 Andrew helped expose the case of Richard Hewitt, a 53-year old man from Birmingham, who was discovered naked and cuffed to the cell bars in the a Thai police station lockup. Following strong publicity, Richard was given proper hospital care and later fully recovered. But it needed major publicity to bring about the necessary action by both the local police and the embassy authorities. The best way to get real embassy assistance is to shed an embarrassing light on its officials or on the government back in London.

Andrew, of course, is controversial and makes enemies easily. He has attacked farang businessmen and alleged property charlatans in Thailand and has in return been threatened with strong retribution including death. His young daughter's school address has been posted on the internet as well as other personal details. He has faced, and still faces, several criminal and civil cases for libel in the Thai courts. None the less, it's worth recording that he has never been accused of a criminal offence outside of Thailand and, within this country, has never yet (at the time of writing) lost a libel suit or any other criminal or civil action. Critics like to point to a famous "Boyztown" libel case of several years ago where, it is true, he was found guilty in the provincial court but was later acquitted in the appeal court where judges concluded that the journalist was simply doing his job in exposing what Andrew claimed to be serious malpractice by a "Scottish McMafia". In 2013 Andrew received the backing of the independent and non-profit making Committee to Protect Journalists, based in New York. The organization exists to defend the right of journalists to report news without fear of reprisal, or worse.

So why don't the Pattaya media normally follow Andrew Drummond into hot territory? It's a question often asked. It's partly to do with the way news is collected. The local media all have reporters who pick up crime stories by following the police going to the crime scene. The journalists then write out what they have been told by investigators. It's a cosy relationship. The press and their cameras are banned from court premises and so can't report proceedings directly. The owners of the Pattaya media don't employ investigators in the western sense and are concerned to avoid libel writs which are easy to serve in Thailand, even if harder to prove in practice. Profits are modest, especially in the print media, and owners are more concerned with paying staff salaries than with being unduly controversial. Andrew Drummond, by the way, is not a rich man by any known measure and openly states that he needs the generosity of his internet readers to remain in the game. But newspapers never receive donations and what matters to media moguls in Pattaya is the support of advertisers. This is reflected in restaurant reviews which are invariably flattering, sometimes to the point of nauseating prostration. The obvious defence, of course, is that readers need to know where to eat and not where to avoid. But don't tell that to the Egon Ronay food guide.

Arising from my embassy and media experience I deduce that there are some simple rules to follow if you are involved in criminal proceedings or just want to buy a property or a business. Beware of lawyers or their foreign "advisors" who want an up-front fee for running your case. Pay as you go. Remember if you pay cash you are never going to get a refund. As the Thais say, the sugar has already entered the elephant's mouth. The worse example I personally ever came across was a 28-year old man from Leeds who was caught with a small quantity of methamphetamines and, through his parents, paid 50,000 pounds to a crooked Thai lawyer and his farang agent for "favours" in the court. When the case eventually came to trial, the lawyer never showed up and is believed to have gone abroad to enjoy his windfall. The poor defendant received six months in jail and the farang agent now resides in Cambodia, I understand, as a property consultant.

It's a sad fact of life that some respectable-looking foreigners offering services in suits and ties are complete rogues. Not all, of course, by any manner of means and that's the rub. Ask around and check people out. Most embassies post a list of suggested lawyers whilst stressing that they can assume no responsibility if matters fail to work out. But don't trust one embassy. See if other diplomatic posts include the same law firm. Long after my retirement, I even had to inform the embassy in the middle of the night that they had recommended on their website the details of two legal practices fronted by foreigners, one who had been disbarred in UK and the other with a pending criminal case in Thailand accusing him of extortion. I suggested strongly to the British ambassador Mark Kent that these particular names be instantly withdrawn or I would return my MBE to London amid a loud fanfare of disgust. I was believed. Two hours later, the embassy authorities had awakened the webmaster (or whoever) from a sound sleep to delete the relevant names.

But I no longer receive greeting cards at Christmas from senior embassy officials.

I recall a British guy who donated several thousand pounds to a blind children's charity in Pattaya, became an official of a local Rotary, could speak passable Thai and even worked voluntarily teaching English to Thai kids. He also set up an agency in Pattaya offering free advice on investments and insurance. But he had spent a secret lifetime financially ripping-off old ladies in UK and depositing his ill-gotten gains in banks in Gibraltar and the Cayman Islands. Eventually he was deported back to UK to face charges of embezzlement, fraud and sex with minors. The long arm of law from UK has got slightly longer in recent years, though many would argue it is still too short. And don't forget that some villains reinvent their biography on the back of an envelope as they fly out to begin life afresh in tempting Pattaya.

There are good, clean and honest lawyers in Pattaya. Sadly there exists the other sort as well.

SEVENTEEN: BODY SNATCHERS AND THE COUP

On the night of September 19, 2006, the Thai army instigated what turned out to be a non-violent putsch against prime minister Thaksin Shinawatra, who happened to be in the United States, and his caretaker government. There had been dozens of attempted Thai coups in the 20th century, the main reason usually cited being alleged corruption by the government on a massive scale. At the time of writing, March 2014, there is speculation of yet another military intervention amid a political crisis which is dividing the country. The Thai word phatiwat (coup) is still one of the most feared in the Thai language. Some of the earlier coups were accompanied by terrible street violence, even including the use of helicopters with spitting machine guns to dispel student demonstrations.

The army tanks rolled into central Bangkok in 2006 without resistance and in Pattaya all was quiet on the military hardware front. The bars remained open as usual even as mobile phones were ringing all over the city for Thais and foreigners alike to gossip about the latest political gamble in the metropolis.

The country was technically under military rule within minutes but in Pattaya a curfew was never on the cards. In the Tahitian Queen, the longest running bar in Pattaya dating back to 1978 in a premier beach front location, the rock n' roll music continued to pump out as beautiful young ladies gyrated for the benefit of all.

I sauntered down to the main police station for my appointment with the Sawangboriboon Foundation, locally known as the Body Snatchers. I half expected to see some coup-related activity in the city's main law and order centre, but not so: the desk sergeant was half-asleep on a quiet evening in the depth of the low season in Pattaya. There was no sign whatever of any out-of-the-ordinary activity except that the terrestrial TV station was playing solemn music rather than the usual diet of Thai soap operas and cartoons. A drunken customer was fast asleep on the floor in one corner of the large reception hall, whilst a foreigner from Sweden was arguing with the traffic section cops about whether he should pay a fine for not wearing his crash helmet when he had just driven to the police station to report it had been stolen.

"This darn country," he muttered in English as he charged out of the police station with his wallet 400 baht (nine pounds) lighter.

The Sawangboriboon Foundation is the Pattaya equivalent of the Bangkok-based Poh Teck Tung Foundation with an ideology based on Chinese beliefs passed down from generation to generation. One of the main tenets is the philosophy of Tai Hong, a respected monk long dead, who had been taking unclaimed corpses to bury at the graveyard. About 100 years ago, Chinese believers in Thailand after a particularly devastating plague began donating clothes, money and coffins and even funded a graveyard for unclaimed corpses. The symbol of the Poh Teck

Tung Foundation is still the Chinese character shan which means the performing of a meritorious deed.

Today in Bangkok, Pattaya and other cities nationwide, the body snatchers operate nightly dozens of privately-owned vehicles and volunteer ambulance teams which park outside petrol stations and burger joints waiting for customers. They listen intently to police scanners, local traffic reports and radio chatter amongst local taxi drivers. They are busiest after midnight, doubtless because alcohol fuels risky driving behaviour, and seldom experience a shortage of business. For example, there are at least four violent crimes and three fatal road accidents reported each hour of the night in Bangkok alone. The figures for Pattaya are lower but still significant enough to warrant a body snatcher presence every single night of the year.

Sawangboriboon had proved to very helpful to me in my ongoing embassy role. They had ferried injured Brits to local hospitals and transported the dead ones to the autopsy centres. They had even arranged the burial of one or two when nobody could be found to pay for a cremation. It seemed a sensible idea to find out more about this charitable foundation whose vehicles with red flashing lights and clearly marked logos were a constant sight on Pattaya's overcrowded roads and streets. It was obvious that the death rate amongst Brits would be higher than it was without a rescue service on 24-hour call. In travels throughout Asia, I never come across such an institution before or since.

I knew that the Thai volunteers had to provide their own gear: uniform, two-way radio, rubber gloves and first-aid equipment, even oxygen tanks although not every unit carried such sophisticated technology. As in any voluntary body, you can be fortunate or not lucky when needing their emergency service. I had several times visited their headquarters in Naklua where a vegetarian two-week festival is hosted annually on behalf of the resort. It's now one of the most popular non-sporting events for foreign tourists in the calendar. But I was curious. In all my experience, I could never once recall the volunteers asking for payment which was a highly unusual state of affairs in Pattaya. Wanting to dig further, I asked the Sawangboriboon head office if I might accompany a group as they went about their work on one evening. Coincidentally it turned out to be the night of the coup.

I was introduced to the team leader Khun Thongchai. He told me that the foundation had been operating in Pattaya for about 15 years, adding that the rise in tourist numbers meant that more people were getting injured and dying here, an encouraging trend from his perspective. He added proudly that he personally had persuaded the local mortuary to expand the number of holding fridges, including a special facility for the unusually obese who exceeded 130 kilos or thereabouts on their demise. He passed the comment that English tourists were very welcome in Pattaya because they drank a lot. Khun Thongchai then suggested I get into the back of his large vehicle with several members of his team and wait for something to happen.

We didn't have to doodle for long. The first call, overheard on the police radio, was news of a car and motorbike accident on Sukhumvit highway on the way to Bangkok. With red lights flashing, the driver put his foot down hard on the pedal and the speedometer rose to over 100 kph. Thongchai explained that it was very important that we got there before any other body snatchers from another company who might also have heard of the tragedy. I was learning already that this was a highly competitive business. In Pattaya proper there is no problem as

Sawangboriboon has a monopoly function, but this is not the case as you head out into other districts. Even fights have been known to break out amongst competing charitable organizations, resulting sometimes in injuries which require hospitalization. On one occasion a volunteer had actually been shot dead. Tragically the body snatchers even have to ferry their own dead in the wake of an angry confrontation.

The accident in this case turned out to be serious and two people had been killed in a head-on collision with another seriously injured, all Thais. The scene was not a pretty one with body parts scattered. The police conducted a brief on-site investigation into the crash and took graphic photographs before two other Sawangboriboon ambulances turned up to help with the transportation. Our vehicle made its way back at high-speed to Pattaya where we deposited a very ill young man at the doors of Banglamung public hospital. Thongchai said that injured Thais were usually taken to public hospitals for emergency treatment as it was unlikely they could afford the costs in the private institutions. He explained too that some private hospitals paid a substantial fee for receiving an injured foreigner, even up to ten thousand baht (around two hundred pounds) if it was clear the victim was wealthy or had good travel insurance. The stiff competition was beginning to make sense.

Our next call came from a Thai lady in Jomtien who had phoned Sawangboriboon directly. She explained that her cat and four kittens had mysteriously disappeared in recent days and that the population in the hen house was steadily going down. Then her husband noticed a 20-foot long Burmese python sleeping most happily in the rafters of the family home. Thongchai phoned Sawangboriboon headquarters to bring snake-catching gear in the form of a long stick, a hook and a large cage.

The reptile, after a brief struggle which it seemed resigned to lose, was accommodated in a new temporary and escape-proof home and promptly returned to a deep slumber. It was later released into a local forest. Apparently, this socially-useful extension of the work of the body snatchers is a much needed service as snakes are still turning up on a regular basis even in the concrete maze of central Bangkok.

Other similar animal-related achievements in Pattaya have included rescuing a stray cow which had sat down in the middle of Thepprasit Road, a busy thoroughfare, and refused to budge. No farmer ever claimed this particular beast. Sawangboriboon volunteers also sawed the tusks of a naughty elephant which had escaped from its pound and was demolishing local houses and businesses in its desperate search for something to eat. The sawing was not really a punishment, more a way of reducing anger and tension in the pachyderm and perhaps also amongst the homeless its actions had created.

With the next call, I was more lucky if that is the correct phrase. A German tourist had been found hanged in his hotel room in central Pattaya. Thongchai used his considerable clout in the organization to ensure that our ambulance, rather than any other Sawangboriboon volunteer vehicle, handled the matter. The police were already there making the customary brief report. Also present were several Thai reporters from the local media. Farang deaths are more newsworthy than Thai presumably because they are less frequent. The contorted body was removed from a hook on the bedroom door but I was then asked to leave the room whilst a search of his possessions was made. I noticed later on that his gold signet ring was missing when the body arrived at the mortuary. Stealing the property of the dead is sometimes a perk of the job. Maybe this explains why, in 12 years of embassy service,

I never saw a corpse in the mortuary with any jewellery still intact or a wallet with more than a paltry sum inside.

Some weeks later I was invited to an exhumation ceremony at the headquarters of the Sawangboriboon Foundation in Naklua. I learned beforehand at the vegetarian breakfast that the organization receives many donations especially in the form of expensive equipment such as specially adapted ambulances as well as basic needs including coffins and communication radios. Many of the resort's wealthy business community recognize that the foundation is providing a much-needed role which is not covered by the existing agencies of the state. Nor are their activities restricted to the Pattaya area. In the floods of 2011, which affected Bangkok and much of northern and central Thailand, Sawangboriboon volunteers delivered large amounts of donated food and provisions to isolated or trapped communities, often by small boats in treacherous conditions.

After breakfast we moved on to the local Pong temple and also a Chinese cemetery with one area reserved for those who died without any relatives to care for them. The foundation's volunteers wore white robes and an orange cloth to ward off malevolent spirits which are believed to lurk wherever death lends a hand. The macabre ceremony is held every few years to exhume the bodies of hundreds of people, including a few foreigners, who died without any relatives to take care. The main purpose is to lay the souls at rest and to allow the volunteers to make merit, but a further reason is obviously to make way for new arrivals. In an elaborate ceremony involving silver daggers, ornamental knives and cleavers which only a good Buddhist would completely understand, the funeral site was dug up and the various bones laid out on white cloths to assist in the cleaning which was done with toothbrushes.

Prior to a mass cremation the skeletons were covered lightly with talcum powder and 20-baht banknotes placed in the lower part of the skulls in a ceremony eerily reminiscent of the ancient Roman practice of placing a coin in the mouth of the recently deceased so that they might pay the boatman Charon who would ferry them across the river Styx to their destiny in the after-world. In an aside typical of Amazing Thailand, I noticed that one of the skeletons had a lighted cigarette placed between its decayed teeth. I couldn't help wondering if the anti-smoking lobby might want to make illegal the inhaling of cigarettes even after you have shuffled off this mortal coil.

Khun Thongchai told me that he always participated in exhumations of this sort and had a very special reason for doing so. He explained that at one such ceremony the spirits of three dead children had appeared before him in a playful mood and refused to keep quiet. Thongchai scolded them and stressed that he would not lay them to rest if they insisted on being a nuisance. On hearing this, the children apologized profusely for their bad behaviour on a public occasion which was being held for their own good. Before disappearing the children promised they would reward Thongchai for his kindness and assistance. Lo and behold, the very next week he won a major prize in the national lottery.

Amazing Thailand indeed.

EIGHTEEN: HAVE YOUR PASSPORT READY

The Thai immigration police are responsible for the security of the country as far as foreigner visitors are concerned. Officials at airports and border posts check passports and visas on entry and at exit whilst immigration offices nationwide keep an eye on aliens whilst they are here. There are also investigation sections to detect and, if necessary, arrest foreigners who are breaking the immigration rules, for example working without an authorized permit or overstaying their visas.

In a typical year nearly three million people enter Thailand illegally or overstay their visas. Most are migrant workers (especially from Cambodia and Mynamar), victims of human trafficking, asylum seekers or refugees. Economic migrants from neighbouring countries do not need to be processed through the court system. The immigration bureau simply deports them, usually in large groups, back to their native border by non-stop bus. Many of them in the Pattaya area are recruited in Cambodia and Mynamar, often to work in the construction industry as labourers, but the organizers and agents somehow always seem to slip through the arresting net. It is common for the same people to return again and again, sometimes in family groups and with babies in tow.

Immigration matters for tourists are always high-profile in the English speaking media in Thailand. Blog sites such as Thaivisa.com, the most widely read and influential, have endless threads advising people, usually Europeans, what to do in a particular situation. Inevitably, some of the replies are wrong and it's not always an easy task for the humble reader to sort the truthful wheat from the incorrect chaff. To make matters worse, the Thai authorities shift the goal posts from time to time which naturally adds to the confusion. Keeping abreast of the latest moves by the immigration bureau is rather like following the unfortunate Sisyphus, in ancient Greek mythology, who was forever doomed to try to roll a boulder upwards to the top of a hill. Somehow he never quite managed it.

Into this maelstrom I decided to hurl myself early on in my embassy career. Brits were continually phoning up and asking me how long an extension they could obtain on this visa or that, how often and why they needed to report their residential address in Thailand, how they could obtain a retirement visa and countless other technical issues about which I knew next to nothing. In 2006 the Thai government of the day overhauled the whole visa system. For example you were now limited to three visits to Thailand in a six months period if you did not have a prior visa obtained at a Thai consulate or embassy abroad. These particular restrictions, by the way, no longer apply.

Two subjects above all others kept re-occurring. Firstly there was the problem of overstay. What happens if you leave the country after the visa date in your passport has expired? The immigration rules simply state that the fine is 500 baht a day up to a maximum of 20,000 baht (four hundred pounds). But what happens if you can't pay or have an overstay problem of several months or even years? The second most important issue constantly being brought up was working in Thailand. Who needed a work permit and why? What happened if you didn't have one? What about voluntary work without any payment?

It was these concerns that led me to open an embassy "office" in a coffee shop in the car park of the Pattaya immigration service in Jomtien in 2006. Both my bosses in the embassy at the time and the then superintendent of Pattaya immigration thought it was a good idea. I was also allowed by the embassy to offer some notarial services to British nationals, in particular doling out forms and issuing income verification letters which were often required to obtain a long-stay visa in Thailand. In the three years that the coffee shop "office" operated (2006-2009), I physically saw over 4,000 Brits for one reason or another and collected in consular fees for the notarial services nearly five million baht. Without ever intending to, I had founded a highly successful business enterprise.

The details of the labyrinth of immigration issues lie well beyond the confines of this book – practices vary in different immigration bureaux in the land in any event – but a review of a couple of cases may illustrate the day-to-day issues of concern. William was a 55 year old naive Brit, a Liverpool bricklayer who preferred to work cash-in-hand, who had come to Thailand on holiday for the first time. He met a young Thai woman, fell in love and been financially skinned alive for his trouble. He ended up completely destitute on the streets of Pattaya not knowing what to do. At our meeting I explained the obvious – the embassy never pays bills – and that he needed financial assistance to get home. He did have a brother in Southport who, having being contacted by the embassy at William's request, did send through Foreign Office channels a thousand pounds.

William's passport showed that he had seven months of overstay in Thailand. I bought him from his available funds a single return air ticket to UK, told him to keep 20,000 baht in his back pocket to pay the maximum fine at the airport and hoped for the best. It worked. He was allowed to board his flight. Of course if he had been arrested for any reason before his brother's largesse arrived, say for stealing food or for vagrancy when he was destitute, he would likely have needed to serve a jail sentence first. He would have ended up at the huge immigration detention centre in Bangkok where all foreign prisoners who are awaiting repatriation must sojourn. But William's tale illustrated to me that Thai immigration laws in practice are not as universally harsh as often depicted. If you have the money, the authorities have a great deal of discretion. The rich are seldom found behind bars.

A second example reflects that matters aren't always so straightforward. Tom was a 63 year old retiree, a former teacher in Doncaster, who had fallen in love on holiday in Pattaya and married the woman of his dreams. The marriage had worked out satisfactorily and Tom spent his early months of retirement here playing golf, visiting Pattaya bars, joining numerous quizzes and playing darts every Friday evening. But, as often happens, he began to feel bored. What could he do? He tried applying for teaching jobs in several local schools but made no progress, probably because he was getting on in years, had no Thai-recognized teaching qualification and was without contacts in the local education system. But his Thai wife ran a small general store and eatery in north Pattaya, with two tables outside for any passing drinkers, and he started innocently chatting to customers and even serving them whilst his wife took a nap or went to visit her ailing mother in Bangkok.

One day the undercover immigration police visited the bar and took a photo of him serving a customer and giving change. Escorted to the immigration police headquarters, he was told he needed a work permit for this sort of activity. His wife was duly summoned and she expressed amazement that her husband had broken the law as he was simply helping in a family concern. It transpired that a nearby Thai-owned business in north Pattaya had reported William as they were jealous that he was drawing customers away from them. Immigration officers asked me to explain to William what the problem was. I advised him to obtain a lawyer, make an apology based on his ignorance of the law, and hope to pay a fine as a warning rather than be prosecuted and deported. William turned out to be luckier than most. His lawyer stitched up a cash deal costing 100,000 baht and the fortunate Brit resumed playing rather bad golf and racking his brains at the general knowledge quizzes which are heavily populated by Brits throughout the city.

I was also asked by the immigration superintendent of the time to assist inside the Jomtien office by taking some of the strain away from the information desk. On a casual basis, I began advising people of various nationalities what forms to fill in to extend their visa, what documents they needed for a one-year visa, how to apply for a Thai driving licence and a dozen other matters which recur when foreigners meet official Thai bureaucracy. In this way the links between the embassy and the immigration bureau grew and I like to think it was to the mutual benefit of both. After I retired from the embassy in 2010, I accepted an offer to continue working at the immigration bureau and this arrangement lasted until early 2013 when I finally realized that it was time to take stock of my life. I needed some time to write this book, see more of south east Asia, improve my bridge and concentrate on a consultancy for a local business enterprise.

But not all my work at the immigration bureau in later years was assisting at the information desk. I was sometimes asked to take reports from foreigners, all nationalities, wishing to complain about other foreigners. Every week I found myself interviewing farang businessmen who claimed that this rival or that enemy was breaking the law by working without a permit or was in serious overstay or was a serial pedophile. It was quite a revelation to me to see just how vindictive some foreign residents of Thailand can about their peers. My role was to take notes, receive any documents or photographs and pass the report to the officer in charge. Needless to say whether any official action followed was never my responsibility.

It has always been my belief that complaints by foreigners at the immigration office were less important than those from Thais. I suspect that the principle is true in any country in the world. However, if the evidence was really strong, I noticed that action would indeed follow. A German man came into the office with a brief-case full of papers. He said he lived in a large Pattaya condominium and knew for a fact that another foreigner living in an apartment there was a major drugs trafficker in the area. There were photographs of the alleged offender apparently dealing in cocaine and full details of his name and date of birth. Even for the overworked immigration bureau, this was a golden opportunity to catch a major offender. That cocaine merchant is now serving a life sentence in a Thai prison.

I mention this case as it was a rare example of a foreigner making a complaint against another for reasons of public spiritedness and because he, and other residents, objected to their condominium becoming a centre for vice. Most of the time, I observed, foreigners trying to make trouble for others are hoping to benefit personally from police intervention. There is even currently a website run by a foreigner inviting people in Thailand to report on their fellow-nationals if criminal activity is suspected. This is presumably an obvious and clumsy attempt by a foreigner to build up a data base on his enemies. Senior police have been informed about this particular example of malpractice.

It is indeed time for Thailand to review its immigration laws as a whole once again. The regional scene is changing fast. At the start of 2016 the 10-nation Asean Economic Community will notionally become a free trade zone – to an extent it already is – and over time this will create a massive mobility of labour and of tourists, just as there has been in the European Union. At first, there will be many restrictions but the barriers will be removed over time. Thailand's labour laws and entry and exit regulations are a myriad of complex rules which don't really fit the new world. Also Thailand needs to import labour from neighbouring countries to compensate for its own shortages thanks to the falling birth rate. In mid-2013 there was substantial publicity about condominiums in Bangkok not being completed on time because insufficient Thai labourers could be found. Meanwhile many Cambodians and Burmese are being deported every month, bussed back to their own borders, because they don't have to requisite documentation to work in Thailand. That's not common sense. Especially as they are often back again the following week.

As regards the traditional tourist and expat markets – let's use the Brits as an example – the Thais could take a leaf out of the Malaysians' book. That country's programme includes a provision that registered retirees have the right to work legally for up to 20 hours a week. Of course, there's a bureaucracy associated with that discretion, but it's a far cry from Thailand and its alien labour laws which outlaw any farang activity, even voluntary work, without a permit. If Thailand were to adopt a strategy along the lines of the Malaysian experiment along with other reforms, such as the abolition of the requirement for long stay aliens to report their address every three months, the resulting good publicity for Thailand amongst potential and existing expats would be enormous.

Thailand cannot take its tourism markets for granted any more even though numbers are currently buoyant (political crises notwithstanding). Its Asean partners are now competing in a big way. Singapore's transformation of its image by the establishment of high-end casinos is just one example amongst many. Hong Kong has a Disney Park of its own. The Philippines have reformed their regulations to make it much easier for foreigners to live in the country without the need for visa runs. Cambodia, an up and coming Asean partner, is seeing tourist numbers exceed its own expectations and the liquor licensing laws are much more user-friendly than here. Thailand has to recognize that in the future it will be challenged in the tourism stakes by her Asean partners.

Reform of the Thai immigration rules is already overdue.

NINETEEN: DECLINE AND FALL

By 2008 the volume of consular business in Pattaya was leading to promises by the embassy that a "proper" office would be opened in the resort. It was said that such a development, to equate with the long-established and pampered British consulate in Chiang Mai, would amount to a recognition that the large British community in Pattaya deserved a better facility than a makeshift operation in a coffee shop. It was also noted in high places in the embassy that one in three of all British consular cases in Thailand as a whole originated in the Pattaya area. That's a third of all hospitalizations, deaths, crises and miscellaneous requests including passport renewals and notarial services. Compared with Pattaya, Chiang Mai was a backwater in case-number terms.

Meanwhile the coffee shop office, located in a unit in the Jomtien immigration car park, was acquiring its own reputation as a rather bizarre yet welcome development. The restaurant proprietors were delighted with its progress and estimated that at least 40 percent of the consulate's customers also ordered a coffee or a beer and sometimes a whole breakfast. The proximity to the immigration bureau also meant that we were receiving more and more enquiries about general passport and visa issues for foreigners in Thailand which, the police superintendent confirmed, we were very welcome to sort out as his own officers were extremely busy.

Various nationalities, not only British, began appearing at the consulate including an elderly lady from the Ukraine, wearing a headscarf and Cossack-type boots, who told me angrily she had recently arrived in Thailand with her husband. They had seriously quarrelled which, looking at the hard features staring at me across the table, did not seem impossible. Sadly her spouse had left a scribbled note that morning in the Pattaya hotel which said he was returning to Kiev immediately and taking the wife's passport with him as he had met a Thai woman in a bar and wanted to spend the rest of his life in contentment. I reassured her that a Thai citizen would never be able to enter the Ukraine without a prior visa and that this permission would be far from easy to obtain. Luckily all ended well and the Thai husband was back in the Pattaya hotel by tea time the same day.

He had indeed been to Bangkok airport with his new lover, but the immigration officer had refused to believe that a 23 year Thai go-go dancer was the same person as in the passport photo which showed a rather cranky-looking, elderly woman who was born in Kiev just after the Second World War. So the Ukrainian veteran and his temporary Thai girl friend had returned to Pattaya in a taxi, their attempt at international emergency migration having been foiled. The go-go dancer had received from the guy 10,000 baht (two hundred pounds) for her time-wasting journey but was more than satisfied with her encounter. After a search throughout the city for new consular premises lasting several months – one possible venue was turned down on the ground that the lift was too small and another because a street dog bared its teeth menacingly when the visiting British health and safety officer approached – senior embassy officers agreed to recommend a tiny 20 square metre rentable office in a block of shop-units in Jomtien soi 5, very close in fact to the immigration bureau and the effervescent coffee shop. I managed to obtain from the unit owner a reasonable rent of 15,000 baht (300 pounds) a month, payable annually in advance. There was a very detailed lease which included mention that the landlord was not responsible for any damage which might occur during a fire, armed robbery attempt, civil commotion or a riot which made me wonder if he knew something I didn't.

Certainly the office wasn't ideal, being too small and having no access to a water supply or toilet facilities. But the embassy stated categorically that this tiny space was all that the cash-strapped Foreign Office authorities in London could afford. In those days Jomtien soi (street number) 5 was prone to flooding and, in the wet season, the muddy waters lapped alarmingly at the entrance. The Foreign Office in London sent out a succession of inspectors who dropped the bombshell that were 10 governmental criteria for opening a provincial, consular office and this particular proposal satisfied none of them. For example, there wasn't a specially provided undercover car park and the traffic on the road outside was too heavy to meet the "quiet suburban" stipulation.

Apparently, some official in London worried that a terrorist might throw a bomb at me or steal the British government's money just as I was cashing up and preparing to go to the bank. Of course, malevolent individuals could have attacked me anytime at the totally unprotected coffee shop. It always struck me as odd that a British government which was obsessed with health and safety regulations allowed one of their representatives for years to walk around with his pockets stuffed with Treasury cash and without any physical protection of any kind whatsoever. For a time I did carry a carefully-concealed pepper spray but abandoned it after accidentally gassing myself during a routine check to see if there was any liquid left inside. There was indeed.

It was beginning to look as if the "proper" office might never see the light of day. Then some bright spark in the embassy pointed out that there was a regulation that if a provincial consular officer collected more than 100,000 baht (two thousand pounds) a month in fees and charges, he or she must be provided with the benefit of secure premises. It was also revealed that the 10 tedious criteria for opening an office could be disregarded if a senior health and safety official decided to issue "a non-compliance certificate of approval". Although there were further scraps and last-minute holdups, including an accident during a storm in the South China Sea in which the specially-imported bullet-proof glass was damaged and had to be replaced, the "proper" office finally opened in January 2009. My part-time Thai assistant was upgraded to full time status to deal with the computerized accountancy procedures which automatically followed in the wake of a new bureaucracy.

The "proper" office boomed and within 12 months was regularly taking 350,000 baht (seven thousand pounds) or more every month in fees and charges. However the embassy decided that I as the honorary consul must no longer be the line-manager for the Thai assistant. She was to report directly to a Bangkok-based officer for reasons of protocol. This mechanism was apparently to deal with the rule that honorary consuls were not supposed to supervise other staff, especially ones involved in finance. This seemed to me rather bizarre in view of the vast sums of money I had handled without incident in the previous few years at the coffee shop, but rules are indeed rules as we all know. I was even discouraged from opening the office at all if the Thai assistant was absent for any reason which frequently happened as she was often summoned to Bangkok for specialized training in computerized systems. In practice I sometimes ignored the instruction not to open and carried on regardless so as not to inconvenience the public.

One day I was shown by an embassy official a memorandum from London that honorary consuls should work only between 6 and 10 hours a month and that, if this guideline was broken, there would need to be a consular review. This again seemed surprising to me as I had long worked in excess of 30 weekly hours and had even been congratulated by a former British ambassador David Fall for that level of commitment. What my boss was really suggesting was that I concentrate on the mortuaries, the hospitals and the jails and leave the office work to the Thai assistant. This would have been fine if only the office had been sufficiently staffed. Of course, it wasn't. The personnel structure was turning out to be wholly inappropriate for a busy office.

By the beginning of 2010 I was feeling it was time to leave the British embassy. Although the "proper" office was proving to be a huge success, I found the stresses and strains becoming too great. There was nobody officially to cover for the Thai assistant when she was on leave or attending meetings in Bangkok. I found it difficult working with a new regime in Bangkok and I sent an email indicating my wish to retire. Consul Gordon MacCleod replied that he thought this was the right decision and reminded me that my contract expired later that year in any case. He made the fair point that he didn't really want to offer another five year contract to a man who was already 68 at the time. Ambassador Quinton Quayle remarked to me that he had no strong feeling either way about my retirement which was a diplomatic way of saying he certainly did. They were looking for somebody new. I had absolutely no problem with that. I adjudged my time had come.

There was a separate set of reasons for me to believe this was the time to quit. Many changes were occurring in the Foreign Office which affected all the overseas missions. The new watchword was standardization, namely to try and make sure that any British national in trouble abroad would receive exactly the same level and quality of service no matter where in the world he or she happened to be. In my last few months, I and every other consular officer in the world had to fill in forms galore to try and prove we were abiding by the new guidelines. There were even attempts to instruct me about hours of working and, when I complained, I was told "you must switch off your mobile phone after four o'clock in the afternoon". Other directives ordered me to reduce the amount of prison visiting and to stop over-servicing the clients. It was no longer a needs-led service in my book. Yes, it was indeed time to go.

Meanwhile the British government was busily clipping the wings of the Foreign Office and its embassies worldwide. The actual scope of embassy authority was actually on the decline and markedly so. The bureaucracy of visas for Thai nationals seeking entry permission into the UK had already been outsourced to VFS Global whilst many of the real decisions were being taken by the newly-created Borders Agency in England under Home Office (not Foreign Office) control. Contrary to what many people continue to think, British embassies no longer have a serious say in who can visit the UK on longer-term visas even though the applications may be lodged there.

Then another blow. In March 2010, the embassy in Bangkok and all those throughout Asia stopped issuing regular passports to British nationals. From now on applicants anywhere in Asia had to apply to the British High Commission in Hong Kong. It was then announced that, from early 2014, all passport offices worldwide would close and applications would need to be sent by customers direct to London and nowhere else. Needless to say, the real agenda for these changes were to cut staffing and to reduce costs. Financial axes are usually swung by people proclaiming to represent the public interest.

An advertisement for my replacement appeared on the embassy website in March 2010 and, I was told, attracted 31 applicants. I was not involved in the selection process which was delayed because of the red-shirt riots and the burning of a central part of Bangkok in April of that year. The announcement was made in due course that my successor was to be Howard Miller, a well-known and successful British entrepreneur who ran a local TV station and internet news channel Pattaya One and later branched out into local real estate. Howard also ran the Foreign Tourist Police Assistants in Pattaya and had achieved a lot of international publicity with the TV series Big Trouble in Thailand which is still today being aired in many languages round the world.

Howard and I were on amicable terms and I hosted an Italian meal for him on the day of the announcement of his appointment. I did confide that I was mildly surprised at the outcome of selection process as a common criticism of me had been that I was too close to the police and the local media. Yet here was a guy who was far more prominent in these roles than I ever would be. After familiarizing himself with the work of the honorary consul and watching the operation of the "proper" office, Howard took over from me at the start of July 2010. My very last embassy case on June 30 was a phone call from a guy who said he was imprisoned in a small room somewhere in Pattaya after confessing to a taxi driver that he didn't have any money to pay for the fare. I suggested that he should ask his jailor to phone me to see if we could help. About 15 minutes later the desperate individual phoned to say he had just remembered he had hidden a 1,000 baht note (20 pounds) in his sock and was now free and on the street.

All's well that ends well. Or so I thought.

TWENTY: PREMATURE BURIAL

When I handed over the consulate keys to Howard Miller, I assumed (as he did) that would be the end of any British embassy involvement on my part. But it wasn't quite like that. Howard threw himself into the post of honorary consul with thoroughness and enthusiasm.

I even received an email from the consular directorate in London wishing me well for the future and stating, in more elegant terminology, that Howard's appointment was the best recent news since the invention of sliced bread. Meanwhile I had transferred to the nearby immigration bureau as an information assistant, so we kept in touch.

He told me that the Foreign Office rules and regulations were becoming tighter and tighter. Less discretion was being invested in individual officers in embassies and consulates as the government marched towards conformity for the treatment of consular cases in nearly 200 countries. You were now required to fill in a form even for the performance of even the mildest of duties. I smiled to myself thinking I was well out of that particular pot.

But within a year or so, Howard was no longer working for the embassy. He departed in some understandable anger. It had long been mooted that the Pattaya office required another full time officer in addition to the Thai assistant, appointed in my time, who rather bizarrely reported in line management terms to Bangkok officers and not to the Pattaya honorary consul. In the summer of 2011 the full-time post of Pattaya-based vice consul, at a salary of over 1,000 pounds a month which compared favourably with the emolument of around 2,000 pounds a year for the honorary consul, was advertised on the embassy website. It was mentioned in the post description that the management of local staff would be an element.

Howard applied for this promotion with a reasonable expectation of success, but the selection panel in October 2011 preferred Leela Bennett, a woman applicant living in London but of Thai parentage. A shocked Howard was offered the opportunity of continuing with the part-time role of honorary consul, but clearly the appointment of someone higher in status than him in Pattaya was too much to bear. He resigned on the spot and has since devoted himself to a successful media and property business in Pattaya. One embassy source confided in me that the biggest argument against Howard's appointment was that he was already running a full-time business which would likely expand in the future and crowd the normal working day parameters for more substantial diplomatic duties. Of course, the selection panel knew all that when Howard had originally been appointed as honorary consul.

As the new vice-consul appointee had to undergo lengthy consular training, her official arrival in Pattaya was delayed for some months. In the meantime the embassy sent down Bangkok-based staff to keep the office open on a part-time basis, but there were frequent no-shows and it became somewhat unpredictable when, or even if, a Pattaya service would continue to operate. Another crisis occurred when the Thai assistant, a left-over from my tenure, was "invited" to resign after a loaded gun was found in her car by a visiting inspector. Regrettably it was an unregistered weapon. It was beginning to look as though the "proper" office was something of a poisoned chalice.

As the consulate was often closed, sometimes for days and even weeks on end, increasing numbers of disenchanted Brits found their way into the nearby immigration bureau. It was common knowledge that I was helping there at the information desk where I dealt with dozens of nationalities and not just the Brits. I informed the embassy of the problem of protesting citizens and the advice of the new consul Michael Hancock was to give out the Bangkok embassy switchboard number for any British consular cases which came my way. In practice it was more difficult than that. When tearful and distressed widows came looking for guidance after their husband had just had a fatal heart attack, or fallen of a roof in unclear circumstances, it seemed unduly churlish just to hand them a phone number, especially when there was no guarantee anyone would pick up the phone, especially on Friday afternoons.

I also dealt with a number of British down-and-outs who had run out of cash and had no friends or relatives to call on for financial assistance. I usually bought these weary guys a breakfast, at my expense, before handing them over to the immigration police for the inevitable overstay offence. They would remain in prison until the embassy arranged for their repatriation, a process which could take months.

Many of the down-and-outs were housed initially at Nong Plalai prison, near Pattaya, and I visited several on my own volition. The guards were highly amused that I was now visiting the prison as a private citizen and not as a consular official, but they kindly allowed me to continue to skip the lengthy waiting period which invariably accompanies visiting hours in institutions run by the Department of Corrections. However, one difference was that the cups of weak tea in the governor's office stopped abruptly. I was even involved in the infamous case of the destitute, sick and homeless Richard Hewitt who was found in Pattaya police cells chained to the bars. He had originally turned up in rags at the immigration bureau in the back of a truck, with a long overstay and a variety of health problems, and I even telephoned the embassy to warn them this case could be troublesome to their reputation. I was right. Only intense media pressure brought about his much-needed hospitalization prior to a hasty dispatch back to UK.

In the new year of 2012, Leela Bennett started her full time vice-consul duties in the Pattaya consulate in a great fanfare of positive publicity and then promptly resigned three months later in April to move on to new pastures. I concluded the selection procedures for this type of post were clearly not infallible. She had no previous knowledge of embassies (as far as I know) nor of Pattaya and its particular consular problems, and was clearly unhappy with the role with a resulting disenchantment which was plain to see. By the middle of the year the Pattaya consulate again became erratic in its hours of opening as Bangkok-based staff, travelling down two or three days a week, tried once again to run a skeleton service to provide notarial services, especially letters for retirees confirming income for the immigration bureau. The situation was clearly unsatisfactory from any point of view. I resumed my role as absolutely unofficial advisor to the increasingly angry British community in Pattaya and spent most of my time trying to explain why the consulate was often closed.

"They are seeking advice from London," was one of my favourite lines. Another excuse was "There's been a mass outbreak of flu in Bangkok."

During that autumn of 2012, there were many rumours about what would happen next. It was claimed that the ambassador was looking for new premises in another part of town. Another suggestion was that the consulate would be relocated to the premises of another European consulate already in operation in Pattaya. One American told me he had inside information that the United States and Britain were about to announce the establishment of an Anglo-American consulate general in the middle of Pattaya's red-light district. Inevitably, too, there were pressure groups lobbying for the re-installation of me which I did not welcome and told them so. Finally the new British ambassador Mark Kent announced that the Pattaya consulate would close permanently on 22 November 2012. The former office was put up for rent and is now a foreign exchange shop.

The ambassador's press release stated that "the embassy is changing the way we provide consular services for British nationals in Pattaya and the surrounding area". No arguing with that. Thus all requests for notarial and documentary services, including income letters for immigration and affirmations to marry, had now to be made to the consular section in Bangkok. Requests for consular assistance, such as prison or hospital visiting or advice in case of someone's death, would also be handled from Bangkok. In early 2013 a new honorary consul Bert Elson, co-founder of the British Legion in the Pattaya area and the host at Tropical Bert's bar and restaurant, was appointed. Bert had been the second-best candidate for my replacement in 2010. However he was a very different official from his immediate predecessors, working for just a few hours a week on instructions from the Bangkok bosses and without a formal base or authority to use an embassy stamp or to sign documents. The honorary post this time was advertised without any salary or reward whatsoever. Maybe that will change once the disastrous history of the Pattaya "proper" office has been forgotten. I suspect, but cannot prove, that Bert has been told by the Bangkok bosses to play a much more subdued role than either Kenyon or Miller ever managed to do. With Bert's appointment, I was at last diplomatically laid to rest.

Looking back now it's clear that the Pattaya consulate was always a doomed enterprise. It was not properly resourced or staffed from the beginning. I always knew that truth but managed to paper over some of the widening cracks during the eighteen months or so I was still the honorary consul. I had been promoted in 2006 partly because I put in more than 30 hours a week and was later criticized because I exceeded just six. It was amusing that the ambassador in his closure announcement in November 2012 pointed out that the premises in any case were too small, had no running water and were prone to flooding in the rainy season. These were, of course, precisely the issues that I had raised prior to the opening in the first place.

The reality is that the experiment had been a failure and that the Foreign Office in London decided to cut its losses and run. However, the money saved on rent and salaries was to be spent on opening a trade office in Vientiane, Laos, or so we were told. The decision to close was actually against a clear trend for European nations to have a raised diplomatic presence in Pattaya. There are currently seven honorary consulates in dedicated premises of their own and there's a likelihood of more to follow. Indeed, the Austrian honorary consul Rudolf Hofer was promoted in new and purpose-built premises to the exalted rank of Consul General of the Republic of Austria in 2012 with full jurisdiction throughout the province of Chonburi. He was even presented with a decree signed by prime minister Yingluck Shinawatra.

However, when one door closes another often opens. Several visa and travel companies in Pattaya now offer the service of taking your British documents to Bangkok on your behalf to obtain that much-needed embassy letter to show the immigration authorities for your one year visa. To be fair, that system is working very well. No need for retirees to go in person to the seat of power in Bangkok's Wireless Road. In Pattaya now you simply go to the private sector. How different this was from the heady days of the 1990s when one consul had warned me, "Don't talk to Pattaya businesses about what we do as they'll try to steal our work."

For some time now the Foreign Office has published a three year consular strategy paper. The first was for the period 2007-2010 and was somewhat wishy-washy. The second covering the period 2010-2013 talks about a "customer-focussed and cost-effective service delivered by a professional and confident global team." But there's also a reference to a "more cost-effective global service" as well as mentions of fewer job opportunities, targeted resources and balanced books" which in everyday language mean financial cuts. Given that Pattaya is only about a two hours' drive from Bangkok, with a regular bus service and taxis on every street corner, it would never have been easy to make out a case for an ongoing "proper" office in such a narrowing financial context even if it had been properly resourced and run. Recently, one retired consular official in Bangkok told me, "If you had not retired in 2010, you would likely have presided over the office closure in any case." Of course, we shall never know.

The most recent three year plan 2013-2016 was published in April 2013 by Foreign Secretary William Haig MP under the awesome title Consular Excellence. He starts by saying he is proud of the many British embassies and consulates round the world but reminds us that they could be better. The key development is the rapid development of digital transformation through social media, with the majority of posts already having Facebook and Twitter accounts. Thus the public will be able to access Foreign Office travel advice on-line at any time together with a revamped system for assisting Brits who find themselves in the middle of a crisis or natural disaster. The latest on-line methods of paying for services before or as you receive them are also being introduced. Haig concludes by saying he wants to ensure the Foreign Office has the best crisis information technology system in the world. It is certainly a far cry from 1997 when the humble fax was the preferred organ of communication. There is also much talk in the document of improving efficiency in the embassies worldwide, increasing stakeholder engagement, use of expert partners, streamlined services and the like.

When working for the embassy I kept the same (privately-owned) mobile phone number for 12 years. After retiring I didn't change it and retain it still. Embassy-related calls to my phone are still not unknown, although I discourage them, but on occasion it is useful to tell callers who are long out-of-date with developments how they can contact the Bangkok mission. I also still receive calls from angry Brits who claim not to have received a reply from Bangkok or London to their urgent email or to have phoned the publicly-promoted embassy switchboard number without ever getting through to an actual person. Anyone calling Bangkok on 02 305 8333 will soon discover the reality for themselves as the pre-recorded messages drone on and on and on. The new order, of course, reflects the truism that the consular service worldwide is geared to helping people to help themselves. That's OK if they have access to a computer. But I sometimes wonder what will happen to those – such as the heart attack victims, the destitute, the recently arrested and the terminally sick – who have suddenly lost control of their lives.

There was an example in late January 2014. An 86-year old retired army man – captain Ronald Edward Webb – was found ill, penniless and disorientated in a Pattaya street. I received a phone call from a concerned citizen explaining that the embassy had refused any assistance on the ground that tax payers' money cannot be used to bail out people who choose to go abroad and can't take responsibility for their own lives. All I could do was to suggest a phone call to Bert Elson, the current honorary consul in Pattaya, who had coincidentally founded the Chonburi branch of the British Legion which retains some clout in the higher echelons of the embassy. Anyway the net result, no matter who was responsible, was that the 86-year old was transferred to a local hospital and rushed into the intensive care unit. As so often in consular affairs involving money, somebody or something has to create a stink to get anything done. That's because it is bad publicity the British government fears the most.

It's odd how the British government formally forbids the "wasting" of taxpayers' money on helping elderly Brits in the Shits, yet spends a fortune of much more dubious causes such as training the army in Mynamar or forlornly tackling the insurgency in Afghanistan. I was told by one of his friends that Bert was personally out of pocket in making efforts to rescue captain Webb. That sounded familiar to me.

It goes with the job Bert!

(Postscript) Whilst this book was being prepared for publication in early 2014, a Select Committee of the House of Commons – seeking opinions on how Britons feel about the assistance they receive abroad worldwide – published a number of the dozens of replies it had received from the general public. A number of the responses unsurprisingly did relate to Thailand and Cambodia, mostly from the dissatisfied relatives of unfortunate Brits who died here in controversial circumstances.

One concerned the drowning of Peter Sinnott in Thailand in 2002. His sister wrote to the Select Committee that they were met with complete indifference from the Foreign and Commonwealth Office desk. The Bangkok embassy apparently assured the family that they had undertaken checks on various hospitals and mortuaries in Thailand but had failed to locate any body. The sister adds that she flew to Thailand and discovered the unidentified body of her brother alongside three other westerners. I recall checking the mortuaries and hospitals in the Pattaya area but, of course, he was not here. In any event, it is the almost universal practice of the Thai police to move farang corpses almost immediately from the provinces to the forensics hospital in Bangkok where autopsies are performed. Peter Sinnott's sister believed then and still believes now that her brother was murdered and describes the service from FCO as a complete shambles.

Rather more well known is the tragedy of Kirsty Jones who was raped and strangled in a Chiang Mai guesthouse in 2000. The parents reported to the Select Committee that they were on holiday at the time and had to find out the circumstances on TV rather than from the embassy. However an officer of the FCO did ring to offer condolences and to ask for Kirsty's insurance details in order to repatriate the body. The parents complain that nobody from FCO ever went to see them and that meetings in UK were always initiated by police and never by consular officials. Their list of grievances also includes disappointment that there was no continuity on the FCO desk with various officers not knowing anything about the case and that there was no information readily forthcoming on inquests, post mortems and repatriation.

A detailed reading of all the Select Committee's release of comments shows that the most persistent complaints are the bureaucratic insensitivity of officials, lack of up-to-date information of the circumstances of a tragedy, failure to follow up with grieving relatives and disappointment with the level of service: one complainant says she was promised that somebody would meet her at Bangkok airport but then told that wasn't possible as the arrival date was a Sunday!

To be fair to the FCO and the embassy, complaints are to be expected in the domain of human misery. It's also true that many embassy officials in Bangkok during my time received accolades from customers who felt they had been treated very well. Indeed, former consular officer Kate Dufall and myself were both awarded MBEs some years ago partly on the strength of our work in difficult cases. The problems lie not in personal fault but in the strict FCO rules which seemingly forbid real-time involvement – embassy officers don't attend court cases, can't spend money or award loans, can't investigate criminal matters, mustn't over-service the customers. And so on.

In fact, of course, the "rules" can be broken depending on who you are and whether you or your loved ones can create a big enough stink. This book has mentioned some such cases. One can only hope that the Select Committee's opening up of the long hidden topic of complaints will lead to clarification of and improvement in the regulations. In particular, the government cannot rely on long accounts on the internet or put too much trust in the social media to replace face-to-face contact. When an emergency or disaster strike, people are looking for reassurance and hard information from a real person.

Even in the 21st century, there are certainly limits to the use of new technology.

TWENTY ONE: ROUND THE WORLD WITH PAPA DOC

It takes all kinds of women and men to make an honorary consul and some hit the ground running. Almost all governments employ them to represent their interests in towns and cities worldwide. In the United States alone there are said to be 1,200 such part-time positions of which the most famous was the short-lived appointment of socialite Jill Kelley who became honorary consul for South Korea in Tampa in the autumn of 2012. She was a prominent player in a national scandal that led to the resignation of CIA director David Petraeus and her credentials were promptly cancelled by the government in Seoul.

This incident and the subsequent allegation that Kelley had tried to gain financially from her post drew a lot of attention to the whole breed of honorary consul worldwide. There was immediate and substantial press investigation of the global institution which concluded that the pay was non-existent, or nearly so, but that the appointees enjoyed status and perks such as doing profitable business deals, speeding through airport immigration lines and the right to the fly the nation's flag on their car. This stands in stark contrast with my own experience in Thailand where I had to stand in line like everybody else and was only allowed to place an embassy sticker on my car when parked on double yellow lines in a genuine emergency. Even this didn't always work and I was towed away on several occasions by a private contractor who was more preoccupied with the 20-pound fine than with the niceties of diplomatic protocol. Once I even had to appear in court on an obstruction charge but was excused by the judge when I proved the large McDonalds beef burger advertisement which had been placed under my windscreen wipers thus obscuring my much smaller sticker underneath.

British author Graham Greene presented a highly negative view of the honorary consul role in his 1970s thriller The Honorary Consul. The character of the title is Charles Fortnum, a British expat serving as honorary consul in a dark region of Argentina near the border with Paraguay where he lives a debased life as a self-pitying besotted, lecherous low-life who abuses his title: the sort of character that the British gutter press may have hoped I was during their investigations of me in 2006. However, the consolation in the book is that Fortnum gets sacked at the end of the tale although why the embassy would have needed a representative in such a remote forest region in any case remains unclear.

Greene wrote an earlier novel The Comedians, set in Haiti, which was turned into a successful film starring Elizabeth Taylor and Richard Burton but featuring in a smaller role Peter Ustinov as the diplomatic representative from Uruguay. The movie concentrated on the evils of the Papa Doc regime and his secret police known as the Tontons Macoute. I happened to find myself in Haiti's capital Port au Prince on a group business trip for an international charity in 1986 when Baby Doc Duvalier, the son of Francis Duvalier, was ousted and exiled in a palace revolution which promptly placed one of his generals in the president's palace. There was a good deal of street violence for a few days with white foreigners being attacked in their cars and alarming quasi-voodoo ceremonies taking place with chanting on street corners. Our hotel manager told us that there was an honorary British consul in Port au Prince and even produced the phone number. Answering the call after numerous abortive attempts, this guy – whoever he was – said in broken English there was not much he could do but advised us to wear a basin over our head if we ventured outside and to sing the praises of one Henri Namphy, apparently the general who had just taken over the country.

Much later, the British government announced in 2012 that the British embassy had re-opened in Haiti after closing in 1966, the very year that the book The Comedians was published. The idea of the new mission is doubtless to expand trade links in the Caribbean rather than to counsel Brits cowering in a hotel basement.

Whether there really was a British honorary consul during Baby Doc's ouster remains a mystery to this day. I doubt it. We eventually made it to the city airport in an ancient bus riddled with bullet holes down one side and protected only by a solitary member of the former presidential guard in a T-shirt and short pants. He was hoping to escape to the United States with a brief case full of American dollars. The woman on the seat next to me on the flight to Miami was a scowling female with thick spectacles but without makeup and attired in a paramilitary jacket and fatigue trousers. She drank heavily and poked at her microwaved meal. Whilst I was on a toilet visit, the stewardess whispered to me not to try to engage my aloof neighbour in conversation as she was Madam Max Adolphe, the fleeing former head of the dreaded Tontons Macoute under both Papa and Baby Doc. I am probably the last person alive who knows that the last head of the Haitian secret police drank her whisky neat and hated underdone steak.

At any one time there are around 270 British honorary consuls in office round the world. They are not all the same. Some are in post essentially to boost commerce and assume the role because of their extensive business contacts. Others have been pillars of the community for a large chunk of their life, for example the remarkable Moya Jackson who retired in 2013 after 25 years in post on the island of Cebu in the Philippines. We shared an hotel some years ago on a consular update course in Kuala Lumpur which included a case study of a serious bus accident with fatal consequences in some God-forsaken place off the beaten track with the local phone lines all down, the internet still a distant dream and the local hospital desperately short of medical supplies during the heavy monsoon rains. I was always grateful that nothing like that actually occurred in or near Pattaya.

In 2009 the British embassy in Thailand announced it was accepting applicants for the new honorary consul position in Chiang Mai in northern Thailand. This move followed the end of an awkward decade-long policy which saw the automatic appointment of the head of the British Council, usually educators who rotated into Chiang Mai every couple of years with no personal ties or vested interest in the city. Previously the government had also experimented with full time diplomats hoping they could encourage trade and investment between the UK and Thailand. The latest appointee was Ben Svasti Thompson, a dual national and long term resident of Chiang Mai who was chosen after a lengthy screening process.

"Initially I wasn't interested in the job," Ben told City Life magazine, "but then I realized it was about social work which is what I have dedicated my life towards. Problems faced by British nationals are health, encounters with law enforcement, making sure their rights are respected and obtaining assistance, especially with the growing number of retirees."

Ben has been and is a very active worker for disadvantaged groups in Chiang Mai, particularly aids sufferers and trafficked or abandoned children. He ought to enjoy a long reign diplomatically in Chiang Mai if he chooses.

On another front Richard Brown, an Italian speaker who has been an honorary consul in Sicily for more than 20 years, is a typical example of the best of the breed. He told The Guardian newspaper, "When they asked me to be the honorary consul, they told me it wouldn't take up much time – all I had to do was to fly the flag a couple of times a year. I said yes, and the next day I was dealing with a couple of Brits who'd been nicked for smuggling seven-and-a-half kilos of hash."

He says that being self-employed is important in the role as you have to have control of your own time in view of the fact you are never quite sure what will happen next. One of his most bizarre cases was when two British tourists, who did not speak a word of Italian, left the contents of their rucksacks at what they thought was a launderette for a service wash costing a couple of pounds. In fact it was a dry cleaners and the bill was nearer seventy pounds. Thinking they had been ripped off they put the equivalent of two pounds on the counter and rushed off with their clothes, only to be arrested in the ensuing chase and commotion. Prosecuted, they faced seven years in jail all because of some dirty washing. A lawyer managed to get them released a few days later for a total cost of 5,000 pounds in fines and compensation. Trivial mistakes can cost dearly and not only in Thailand.

For some reason I can't detect there appear to be more honorary consuls in the Caribbean than you might expect. Ian Court was honorary consul in San Juan, Puerto Rico, for 15 years and wrote a book about his experiences Funny, Stupid and Just Plain Stupid, which recount his experiences "on the 391st rung of the British diplomatic ladder". Ian was appointed in 1986 and soon got used to dealing with anything from lost passports to sunken yachts. His only training, he says, was reading through Graham Greene's novel The Honorary Consul which didn't help much. With a background in theoretical chemistry and an appointment as a American university professor in his early thirties, he used his growing commercial experience to push hard for trade and investment in Puerto Rico. The country had broken into the top 50 markets worldwide by the time Ian retired in 2000, prompting the British government to put in a full consulate. His had become a wider remit than that of most honorary consuls.

Although the most I ever suffered were a few bruises and scratches in the line of duty, working in the diplomatic service can be dangerous. A former honorary consul in one of the post-Soviet "Stans" had his car tyres slashed and a crude warning placed on his smashed windscreen after he appeared in court for the prosecution and against a local self-styled Mafioso. He even received a letter advising him to expect a horse's head to turn up in bed beside him although no dead creature mercifully ever appeared. In 2009 John Terry, an honorary consul for the British High Commission in Jamaica and long-term resident there, was found lying dead on his bed with a cord round his neck and severe head injuries. There was a handwritten note on his corpse describing him as a "batty man" which is local slang for a homosexual. Police assumed it was a homophobic attack since there was no sign of robbery or forcible entry to the premises. A 23-year old local man was later charged with conspiracy to murder.

In fact the history of consular representation is littered with morbidity. The function seems to have originated in ancient Greece when the Proxenas, usually rich merchants, helped out people of their own city state who found themselves in trouble abroad usually because of a commercial dispute. According to the blind poet Homer, one such volunteer was hacked to death by the Trojan mob on hearing that the Greeks had set sail to attack them following the abduction of Helen. The Romans also made use of honorary officials to assist the consuls who were the most important officials of both the Republic and the Empire. The ancient historians tell of a Roman diplomat in Parthia who was nailed to a door and given the death of a thousand cuts after being impolite and accidentally insulting his host by vomiting at a banquet.

During the heady days of the Ottoman empire, a French king sent an envoy to Constantinople to request that the Turkish armies should cease their siege of Vienna in 1683. However, the Sultan was not best pleased and sent back a small part of the consul's body to Versailles, his head to be precise. In nineteenth century Germany, the position of consul was thought to be so prestigious and dangerous that special privileges were bestowed. The official's wife was known as Consu.ainly no exception to the rule. One of my favourite books has always been Voltaire's Candide which describes a man setting out on a journey who, because of various negative circumstances, experiences one traumatic event after another. Embassy work can be like that – whatever can go wrong for people in a crisis situation often will. But the important thing is to separate completely one's professional and private life. On the rare occasions when I forgot that precept I was sorry afterwards. Voltaire's character concludes at the end, "il faut cultiver notre jardin" which basically means that the only way to survive in a world full of tragedy and difficulty is to focus on your own corner (your garden) and to recognize your own limitations.

When the embassy told me to switch off my mobile phone after four-clock they were quite right. I had learned to recognise my limitations.

AFTERWORD

To be honest, I feel that the best days for the Brits in Pattaya are behind us. The most recent figures show that one quarter of all foreign visitors to Thailand are now Chinese with booming numbers from other Asian countries and eastern Europe, including Russians in particular. Although the Foreign Office continues to perpetuate the nonsense that there are 800,000-plus British nationals visiting the kingdom annually, anyone who bothers to investigate will discover that the trick is in how the numbers are calculated.

Brits were for many years the largest contingent of any foreign country, but that was before the Russian, Chinese and Indian governments started issuing passports on a gigantic scale in the wake of economic booms of one sort and another. The British presence in Thailand has declined for many reasons. The economic malaise in the European Union and the slump of the pound, the increasingly high cost of living in Thailand especially hospitalization, air fare hikes, the opening up of eastern European cities offering good-times holidays at a fraction of the cost to Pattaya, the diversification of the resort away from its traditional role as a sex hot spot. All these have played a part. In China, a recent survey suggested that half the population wanted to visit Thailand even though only one percent has yet done so. By comparison, Britain's market is, as they say, a "mature" one, if only because its population is miniscule by comparison.

The question is often posed now whether Thailand in general, or Pattaya in particular, is becoming a more dangerous destination. Certainly many features have improved dramatically over the past 20 years. The high quality of hospital care, provided you are properly insured or can afford the best, is now taken for granted. Tourist courts have now been established in Thailand, including Pattaya. They can't try criminal cases – the job of the ordinary courts – but they can take witness statements and adjudicate civil cases where both parties agree. The child sex industry is definitely on the decline as the Thai police and social services network finally get their act together, at any rate as regards foreign perpetrators.

But foreign headlines continue to be created by unsavoury publicity here in Thailand. During 2013, three foreigners sustained gunshot injuries in Chiang Mai when a drunken college student opened fire in an eatery. In Phuket, a Russian man was slapped around and a fake revolver pressed to his head by the jealous boyfriend of a Thai woman he had spoken to. Sexual assaults continue to be widely publicized including the "Evil Man of Krabi" which led to a video clip posted on You Tube by the father of a Dutch teenager raped there.

In Pattaya, the spate of street crimes including bag snatching and various scams continue to plague the resort. Perhaps the biggest threat to tourism concerns the safety of vehicles. Dozens of people, including some foreigners, have lost their life in bus accidents. Safety standards on public vehicles are still way below internationally accepted standards. During my embassy career I visited the site of several bus crashes in the Pattaya area, where Brits were involved, and it was obvious from even a superficial examination that the tyres were bald or that proper mechanical servicing was just a pious dream.

Then there was the derailment of the overnight sleeper train to Chiang Mai in July 2013 in which 23 people, the majority foreign tourists, were injured. Earlier in the year five passengers were killed, including a Belgian woman, when a tour bus plummeted off a winding road in Phitsanulok after its brakes failed. The number of negative media reports, especially back in Europe, prompted the Thai foreign minister to promise that tourist safety is now one of the government's top priorities. The problem lies in translating promises into concrete action.

The tourist police say they keep records nationally of all their tourist complaints and that they are currently averaging 8 or 9 a day. They include mainly reports of missing valuables, documents or thefts from public places and buses. That said, many complaints are recorded by the mainstream police and are not automatically reported to the tourist police division. Until the Thai police force nationally is instructed to keep one master file of tourist complaints, accidents and disasters, it is simply impossible to know the truth. It seems likely, though, that the number of physical assaults on tourists is going up year on year. In response the police say that their manpower is the same even though foreign tourist numbers have doubled in just a few years.

The World Health Organization's global status report on road safety 2013 found that Thailand ranks 10th place in terms of fatal road accidents after, amongst others, India, China, Brazil and the United States. In south east Asia, Thailand is ranked second after Indonesia. Significantly Thailand's fatal traffic accidents have an awesome 74 percent of deaths accounted for by people riding motorbikes. Although alcohol is usually blamed for so many crashes, it also seems that carelessness by tourists plays a significant part. For example, foreign hirers of motorbikes here often don't show a driving licence – a passport will do – and they ignore the reality that the engine capacity of Thai bikes is often much higher than at home. They are in nearly every case riding around at high speed totally uninsured. If Thailand is serious about tourist safety, then the whole business of renting vehicles needs to be addressed in detail. At the moment, a foreigner without a valid licence or insurance simply pays a fine and proceeds on his way.

In Pattaya bay over the years several speedboats have sunk whilst transporting passengers to and from neighbouring islands. The main reason has been poor maintenance of the vessels, overloading or inexperience of the crew. Separately fires in hotels are a frequent worry and are usually the result of faulty wiring. Twelve years ago a British tourist was killed when his parasail landed on the wires of an electricity pylon with catastrophic results. At the time it was promised that hazardous and dangerous sports would be outlawed. But it never happened. Too often the Thai authorities say they will introduce this or that improvement, but the promises are often forgotten when the publicity dies down.

This is not to say that Brits will desert Thailand en masse. By no means, but I suspect that within a few years many UK tourists will visit the country as part of a package now that Cambodia, Mynamar, Vietnam and Laos are opening up in every sense of the word. There is already talk of a Schengen-type visa to cover some or all of the Asean partner countries. On the other hand, the traditional predominance of Pattaya Brits in running restaurants, bars, estate agencies and businesses is likely to decline if only because they are too many of them for the unfolding scenario.

I recently attended a Pattaya expat club meeting at which these matters were discussed. "I run a bar in south Pattaya," said the guy from Cardiff, "and I can tell you that not one Chinese customer has entered my place, not ever." However, he added that several had asked to use the toilet and he now found it necessary to charge the equivalent of 50 pence for the service. "There's more profit than on a bottle of beer you see."

Another guy from Bradford said that he leased a night club on the Walking Street. "When I started here five years ago, the main language amongst the customers was definitely English. Now it's Russian or Arabic. I no longer hang around the bar because nobody is interested in chatting to me like in the past." He added that his club, like many others, was up for sale. "The new tourists from China and Russia aren't interested in go-go joints. Or not interested enough anyway."

It was my good fortune to represent the British embassy in Pattaya in its golden years as regards the British expat and tourist population. Never a dull moment. It's an experience which likely cannot be relived. But that's good news for my successors.

Hopefully, they won't be as busy as I was.

ABOUT THE AUTHOR

Barry Kenyon, a Liverpudlian, gained a first class honours degree in Latin, Greek and ancient history at Liverpool university.

He spent most of his working life in colleges in UK and abroad and claims to have been the last Latin teacher ever employed in Asia.

Living in Pattaya for 20 years, he has had several roles apart from working for the British embassy in Thailand.

He is a former deputy editor of Pattaya Today, a fortnightly newspaper, is the founder of Pattaya bridge club and has held various roles with local police.

He ackowledges the great assistance that staff at Pattaya Today have given in the publication of this book.